NO PLACE TO LEARN

TOM POCKLINGTON AND ALLAN TUPPER

NO PLACE TO LEARN

Why Universities Aren't Working

UBC Press · Vancouver · Toronto

09 08 07 06 05 04 03 02   5 4 3 2 1

Printed in Canada on acid-free paper

National Library of Canada Cataloguing in Publication Data

Pocklington, T.C. (Thomas C.)
  No place to learn

  Includes bibliographical references and index.
  ISBN 0-7748-0878-0 (bound); ISBN 0-7748-0879-9 (pbk)

  1. Universities and colleges – Canada. I. Tupper, Allan, 1950- II. Title.
LB2329.8.C2P62 2002   378.71   C2001-911557-1

Canadä

UBC Press acknowledges the financial support of the Government of Canada through the Book Publishing Industry Development Program (BPIDP) for our publishing activities. We also gratefully acknowledge the support of the Canada Council for the Arts for our publishing program, as well as the support of the British Columbia Arts Council and the help of the K.D. Srivastava Fund.

Printed and bound in Canada by Friesens
Set in Bembo and Trajan
Design: Neil and Brenda West, BN Typographics West
Copy editor: Judy Phillips
Proofreader: Tara Tovell
Indexer: Annette Lorek

UBC Press
The University of British Columbia
2029 West Mall
Vancouver, BC V6T 1Z2
(604) 822-5959 / Fax: (604) 822-6083
www.ubcpress.ca

CONTENTS

CHAPTER I

NO PLACE TO LEARN

This book critically examines contemporary Canadian universities. It argues that their broader purposes are seldom probed thoroughly and critically. Canadian universities are worse off for this neglect. This book outlines our strong disagreement with the priorities of Canadian universities and presents a clear alternative. It criticizes universities' neglect of undergraduate education, challenges their emphasis on specialized research, and rejects their common claim that teaching and research harmoniously reinforce each other. In our opinion, Canadian universities no longer provide effective, high-quality undergraduate education.

Canadian universities are controversial early in the twenty-first century. Important debates are occurring about rising tuition, student debt, and access to universities. Concerns about political correctness in the classroom and in university hiring have attracted public attention. So too have perennial worries about the employment prospects of graduates and the relevance of university education for the workplace. Large numbers of Canadian professors will soon retire, to be replaced by a new generation. The priorities of this cadre of new professors will shape Canadian higher education well into the century. Debates will undoubtedly occur about the proper roles of universities and their new professors. The institution of tenure continues to attract criticism on and, more frequently, off campus. The political obsession during the 1990s with balanced budgets caused governments to think more systematically about universities than they had in the past. Today, Canadian business leaders show unprecedented interest in the operation of universities. The annual survey of Canadian universities by *Maclean's* magazine both reflects and increases public awareness.

That said, debate about Canadian universities is episodic, seldom probing or philosophical. Its terms are increasingly dominated by the universities themselves, which skilfully argue their case. Universities in this country are poorly understood by citizens, by their students past and present, by media, by governments despite substantial public funding, and even by those who work within them. As a result, university priorities are seldom challenged or even debated. Universities, more so than any other powerful Canadian institution, sail on seas of unwarranted deference.

Canadians' general lack of awareness about institutions of higher education should not be surprising. Canadian universities enjoy a privileged position. They are primarily funded by taxpayers yet they enjoy considerable legal and political independence. Such independence is broadly accepted by Canadians and rests on the view that independent universities are integral to the quality of democracy. And while enrolment is increasing at Canadian universities, still only one in four Canadians will attend university. More importantly, Canadian universities are remarkably complex organizations. They undertake specialized research that is important for Canada's economic well-being but which is difficult for outsiders to understand and analyze. Universities teach an array of subjects to diverse students. They also provide public service that enriches society. For these reasons, universities seem remote and imposing.

Modern Canadian universities are internally complex. They are administratively divided into large faculties (such as science, medicine, law, and business) and then into departments, which yield further specialization. Many of the departments – anthropology, biochemistry, linguistics, and hematology to cite a few examples – pursue subjects whose intricacies are far removed from the daily lives of Canadians. Like all powerful institutions, universities employ an insider vocabulary that frustrates external scrutiny and makes difficult public debate about priorities. Universities speak about technology transfer, interdisciplinary studies, and postmodern interpretations of society. Research, the modern university's lifeblood, relies on insider terms such as "dominant paradigms," "peer review," and "research designs."

In the breadth and complexity of its roles, Canadian universities differ from their simpler predecessors and from other large organizations in the public and private sectors. Management theory now asserts that effective organizations must establish priorities and shed activities that distract from their core businesses. Universities reject such advice and relentlessly add new roles. The modern university now sees itself as educator, researcher, and protector of culture and tradition, and, increasingly, as the "major agent of economic growth: the knowledge factory as it were, as the centre of the knowledge economy."[1] As its roles proliferate, the university grows remote from the broader society, unwieldy in its organization and policy making and difficult to hold accountable.

The complexity of the modern university and the breadth of its activities have impressed many observers. Perhaps the most astute analyst is Clark Kerr, former chancellor of the University of California's world-renowned Berkeley campus. Kerr coined the clever term "multiversity" to describe the large universities that emerged in the United States after the Second World War.[2] For Kerr, the university was no longer a simple community of scholars and students united by a search for a deeper understanding of nature and humankind. On the contrary, it was a series of specialized factions, disciplines, students, and research activities united only by occupancy of a common territory called the campus. In the multiversity, natural sciences (biology, chemistry, and physics, for example) are powerful, specialized, and increasingly separate from social sciences (such as economics, sociology, and political science) and humanities (philosophy and languages). The graduate schools, where students pursue masters' and doctoral degrees, compete for scarce resources with the undergraduate programs.

In the multiversity, the major professional faculties, notably law and medicine, are primarily oriented toward their professions beyond the university. They have few relationships with other parts of the university. Universities now house independent research centres that have little or no relationship to teaching. Under university aegis, commercial firms are established and housed on campuses as universities assume new roles in the development and production of advanced goods and services. Governments, corporations, and alumni vie for influence over university priorities. Leadership in the multiversity is highly political. It cannot easily impose an intellectual vision, a common curriculum, or even common standards in areas such as hiring and staff evaluation. Like democratic politicians, university administrative leaders – presidents, vice-presidents, deans, and leading members of boards of governors – broker deals between competing factions.

As workplaces, universities differ from other large organizations. This fact increases their mystique, makes them difficult to comprehend, and magnifies their distinctiveness. The professor's work is unlike almost any other occupation. Her obligation to undertake research is little understood by citizens and, in our experience, by most university students, who see their school as an instructional institution. Professors have remarkable control over the timing, nature, and even location of their work. They enjoy substantial freedom in the courses they teach and in how they teach them, in the subjects on which they undertake research, and in the performance of obligations to their students, their colleagues, and the university. Employment practices such as tenure and sabbatical leaves, although not unique to the university, expand the distance between the university and the society. Professors' deep commitment to their disciplines (primary areas of expertise) is little understood beyond the university. The idea that universities should be run as democracies makes them profoundly different from other large North American workplaces.

THE ARGUMENT IN BRIEF

Three themes dominate this book. First, modern Canadian universities wrongly and seriously devalue the education of undergraduate students. Undergraduate classes are too large, frequently taught by graduate students rather than professors, and often delivered in ridiculously impersonal and uninspired ways. This unacceptable situation has several causes, notably the prevailing view that universities are only partially teaching institutions. According to universities themselves, they are steadfastly committed to research. The corollaries of this view are twofold – all university professors must be teachers *and* researchers, and good research is *essential* to good teaching. These ideas, which took root in the 1960s, are now held as unquestioned truths by the vast majority of university professors and administrators in North America. On both empirical and philosophical grounds, we challenge the idea that teaching and research are mutually reinforcing activities. Our view is that university research often detracts from the quality of teaching. We regret the continuing elevation of research and the systematic neglect of the quality of instruction. At this point, readers are urged to reflect on the following simple observation. In the 1990s, Canadian universities complained about underfunding, about crowded campuses, and about the deteriorating quality of education. Not one of them responded by increasing the teaching obligations of their permanent instructors. In fact, many managed to reduce even further the teaching activities of professors.

Our second theme is that university research, the activity that now outstrips teaching in importance, is often specialized and far removed from the needs of undergraduate students. Canadian universities suffer from their acceptance of research as a higher priority than teaching. A precise rationale for expensive research is seldom provided by universities or debated by the broader society.

We examine the distressingly conformist views in North American universities of the meaning of research, of the measurement of its significance, and of its relationship to national well-being. In particular, we note how Canadian universities now prize research that brings new facts to light. Such research, commonly called frontier research, holds sway. Frontier research has replaced reflective inquiry, a complex process involving disciplined thought about major issues and the quality of existing knowledge, as the dominant concept of university research. Frontier research and new discoveries enjoy unwarranted status. Reflective inquiry is badly undervalued by Canadian universities.

Our third concern is the increasingly close links between universities, governments, and large corporations. North American universities have undertaken economically significant research for most of the twentieth century. For one thing, they provide most of the trained personnel required for a modern economy. University research in science and engineering has been generally, although loosely, allied with national and corporate priorities. To deny this reality is to misunderstand profoundly Canadian higher education. Canadian universities, especially since the Second World War, have been closely linked with national economic and scientific objectives. The ivory tower has long since faded as a reality.

In the 1990s, Canadian universities charted new courses in their dealings with business and governments. They became strongly committed to a particular view of economic development. Canadian universities now advocate the knowledge economy, a set of ideas about modern society and its underpinning economics. The idea of the knowledge economy rests on interrelated assertions about the need for university-based learning as a key to national prosperity, about the need for university-based research in science and computer studies, and about the imperative of retaining within Canada highly educated researchers. In this perspective, such economic factors as natural resources pale in comparison with national scientific and research prowess, high levels of government spending on research, and the sustenance of research universities.

Since the 1990s, Canadian universities have undertaken and promoted partnerships with corporations and governments for the development, marketing, and sale of particular products and industrial processes. Such relationships, which envision universities as economic agents rather than educational institutions, pose complex questions. They further challenge the quality and priority of university teaching. University priority setting is made more complex as higher education becomes intermingled with corporate and governmental policy.

These three basic problems – mediocre undergraduate teaching, an obsession with research, and an increasingly close relationship between universities, corporations, and governments – demand serious assessment of university priorities. To this end, we advocate four key propositions:

1. Universities must re-establish undergraduate teaching as their first priority. Undergraduate teaching must be recognized and valued for what it is: a complex and important activity that demands broad reading, disciplined thought, and great effort.

2. Universities must carefully reflect on the meaning and quality of research. In particular, research should be viewed much more broadly than it is at present. Professors must think about the human condition, embrace the major contributions of other disciplines, and show general knowledge. Universities should frankly admit that much of their research is of poor quality with little relevance or intrinsic merit.

3. Universities must come clean about the relationship between teaching and research. The present view that teaching and research go

hand in hand must be replaced by the more compelling view that teaching and research generally conflict with one another. Both activities, to be performed well, are enormously time-consuming. They involve different skills and impose contrary obligations on professors.

4. Universities must examine how research partnerships with corporations shape the quality and nature of research. Careful consideration must also be given to the impact of such partnerships on overall university priorities. Partnerships that distort university priorities should, if operative, be abandoned or not proceeded with in the first instance.

Before proceeding, we want to be crystal clear about some basic points. First, we are deeply committed to university ideals, especially the principle that independent universities must be sites for the pursuit of truth. We believe that Canadian universities have made major contributions to the quality of Canadian society. On a personal note, university life has afforded us great opportunities for personal growth, intellectual freedom, and fulfilling lives. That said, universities are powerful, independent institutions that require vigorous criticism. Americans, including many distinguished university presidents, have often been highly critical of universities. The vigour of higher education in the United States is undoubtedly partially attributable to this tradition of self-examination. Second, we hold many conventional views. We accept the institution of tenure. And while we call for significantly improved teaching, we also believe that professors must undertake research and publication. In fact, our standards for research would be much higher than present in Canadian universities. Moreover, we see high-quality research, especially in science and medicine, as essential to Canadian well-being. We fully accept that universities are, and must be, sites for outstanding research, whether it be reflective inquiry or frontier research. In the matter of research, we challenge the view that research is, and must be, a fundamental obligation of all professors and all universities. We also believe that large amounts of frontier research are of low quality, minimal relevance, and little long-term value. Third, we do not see universities as ivory towers, distant from the world around them. On the contrary, universities should render thoughtful service to society. Their teaching, to be effective, must be relevant to societal needs. In fact, we argue that good university teaching *always* increases students' employability, albeit often in subtle ways. Finally, we are not impassioned advocates of liberal education. Faculties of Arts, the centrepieces of liberal education, are obviously important. Science and engineering are equally fundamental to understanding the human condition.

This book is unapologetically aimed at general readers. We try to explain how Canadian universities operate and how they *should* operate. We challenge conventional wisdom, pose alternatives, and argue for reforms. We hope professors in Canada (and elsewhere) read this book carefully and reflectively. We also hope they see merit in our ideas and suggested reforms.

BROADER INFLUENCES

We are "insiders" who have spent our adult lives studying and teaching at Canadian universities. We have been graduate or undergraduate students at Queen's University, Carleton University, and the University of Toronto. We have spent our careers as instructors at the University of Alberta with stints at Acadia and the University of Victoria. Insider status undoubtedly brings with it biases and assumptions of which we are unaware. At the same time, we note that modern universities have seldom been explored satisfactorily by outsiders. The most influential scholarship, with almost no exceptions, has been done by university professors or by university administrators. This fact attests to the remarkable complexity of the university as an institution, to the diversity of its goals, and to its distinctive culture as compared with corporations and governments.

As noted, this book does not lament the decline of liberal education, the weakening of traditional curriculum, or the underfunding of humanities and social sciences. These concerns are examined but in the context of the expansion of medical sciences, the growth of engineering in Canadian universities, and the expansion of scientific and professional education in general. Science and medicine, not liberal arts, dominate the modern university, shape its priorities, and determine its relations with society. Reforms that are rooted in nostalgic appeals to the traditions of liberal education are doomed to failure. Nor do we urge a vision of some glorious past that we wish to recreate. Indeed, even a cursory examination of the history of higher education cautions against embrace of a golden age. The nineteenth-century North American college, generally run by an organized religion, has been described as "depressing and sterile."[3] That said, our call for significantly improved undergraduate teaching inevitably appeals to yesteryear for the simple reason that, until the 1970s, undergraduate teaching was the preeminent role of Canadian universities.

In undertaking this study, we became convinced that interpretations of modern universities systematically exaggerate the influence of forces external to the university. They seriously underestimate universities' capacity to shape their own destinies and the broader society. Early in the twenty-first century, critics and supporters see universities as shaped by four powerful external forces, although such observers differ in the weight they attach to each of them. The four powerful forces are business and the capitalist economy, the funding and policy priorities of democratic governments, the imperatives of advanced computer technology, and finally, changing societal expectations and demographics that, seen together, establish a culture of life-long learning. We acknowledge these forces and their importance for higher education. Our view is simply that the university has considerable independence of response. It responds to external forces but also shapes them and society's views about higher education. Large universities do not passively receive society's signals and pressures. They are powerful institutions with priorities, strategies, and philosophies.

Two forces shape Canadian universities' responses to the broader society. First, university policy making is driven by the priorities, interests, and political objectives of their permanent professors. In no major area of academic life have external forces trumped professorial power or preferences. The dominant views of the university – that all its members must teach and do research, that teaching and research are interdependent activities, and that the university is a central part of the knowledge economy – are endorsed by Canadian professors. Moreover, no external body, including government, can easily impose its priorities on a university in the face of concerted opposition of their professors. To this end, readers are reminded that both the Harris Common Sense Revolution in Ontario and the Klein Revolution in Alberta started with ambitious projects of university reform. Neither made much headway in fundamental university reform. Second, the priorities of Canadian universities are heavily shaped by higher education in the United States and by an interuniversity struggle for prestige and recognition. Canadian universities take their cues one from the other and from their American "competitors" rather than from the society at large. They are imitative rather than independent in their policy making. It is for this reason that universities offer almost identical visions of teaching and research.

The philosophies of the large, internationally recognized American research universities such as Harvard, Princeton, the University of Michigan, Stanford, and the University of California at Berkeley are influential in the struggle for university prestige. These universities are the models, the trend-setters in research, the training grounds for future intellectual elites, and allegedly the intellectual heart of the Western world. Their significance is captured by the lament that Canada lacks a single university of their stature and that the national interest suffers as a result. The graduate schools of the elite American research universities (where students do advanced research for doctorates) are particularly influential in defining trends and shaping the policies of other universities. For this reason, major reforms normally begin within an elite American university (or group of them) and move sometimes slowly, sometimes quickly, through the continental system. Innovations in higher education radiate from elite American universities and in this country from the University of Toronto, McGill University, and the University of British Columbia.

Canadian views about universities are heavily influenced by American ideals. In this regard, a unique institution – the American research university – looms large.[4] Even harsh critics admire the undoubted achievements of America's research universities. Leading American research universities are the crown jewels of higher education. They are said to be the vanguards of economic and social progress; successful blends of excellent teaching, research, and public service; and major forces in the intellectual life of the democratic world. They are models, the standard to which others aspire, sources of great American pride, and allegedly determinants of America's world dominance. Such sentiments are partially captured in a recent analysis of undergraduate teaching in American research universities: "Their graduates fill the legislatures and board rooms of the country, write the books we read, treat our ailments, litigate our issues, develop our new technologies, and provide our entertainment. To an overwhelming degree, they have furnished the cultural, intellectual, economic, and political leadership of the nation."[5]

We too admire the achievements of American research universities. But they are not models to be slavishly imitated by Canadians. Moreover, major differences exist between higher education in Canada and higher education in the United States that must be constantly borne in mind. Canadians often hear references to the wonders of major American universities. The reputations of Yale, Princeton, and Stanford are well known to Canadians. In twenty-first-century Canada, their appeal undoubtedly outstrips that of Oxford and Cambridge for young Canadians. However, Canadians know much less about the weak undergraduate teaching that occurs within such universities. They also hear little about the quality of the thousands of lesser American universities and colleges, which educate many more students than the elite universities and which are generally inferior to Canadian universities.

We hope this book is recognizable as the work of professional political scientists. Three themes, heavily stressed by modern political science, shape it. First, modern political science now accepts that governments actively shape, not merely reflect, societal preferences and attitudes.[6] In this vein, we see the modern university as a political force that aggressively shapes its environment. Universities like to convey an image of weakness. They seldom mention their close links to governments and corporate leaders, their capacity to create demand for their services, and their remarkable freedom from systematic examination by mass media. Second, we see Canadian universities as political systems whose major problems must be addressed as political issues. Why, for example, are undergraduate students the weakest group in the university even though numerically they are the largest group, even though they provide large amounts of operating revenue through tuition fees, and even though their education is widely thought to be at the heart of the university's mandate? Why do university administrators and professors lament their diminished status and the declining quality of their institutions when outside observers see universities as powerful economic forces? Why is the modern university simultaneously criticized for being too distant from and too close to the broader society? Such questions are clearly political ones and are addressed as such. Finally, our study is driven by a strong desire to reform the university. Reforming zeal is well known to political scientists who have long worried about the quality of democracy. Like democracy, higher education evokes strong emotions and differing viewpoints.

Despite the critical tone of this book, we are not pessimistic about the future. Universities, despite their embrace of tradition and despite their image as never-changing institutions, actually change frequently and quickly. Nothing in the history of universities suggests a clear, inevitable path for their development. While we see no quick demise of the research imperative, it may well recede to be replaced by a stronger commitment to serious undergraduate teaching. We outline a number of possible developments in our conclusions.

METHODOLOGY

This book rests on a methodology with three strands. First, we studied the literature on higher education in Canada. We quickly concluded that this literature is very sparse and heavily influenced by the vast American material on higher education. We then immersed ourselves in the American literature and studied its major works. Much of our time was spent reflecting on the issues raised and thinking about their implications for Canada. In this sense, we tried to practise the reflective inquiry that we preach. Second, we undertook interviews with faculty members at several Canadian universities.[7] These were done to get a feel for faculty concerns and priorities at several universities and in a number of different disciplines. Finally, many of our arguments are inspired by our experiences as professors over the last two decades. Our views are shaped by thousands of conversations with students and colleagues at many universities, by participation in university decision making at various levels, and by observation of different universities in Canada and occasionally in other countries. A particularly influential experience was team-teaching a senior undergraduate class on the Canadian university on two occasions in the mid-1990s. Through those courses, we had an opportunity to reflect on many of the issues we are writing about and to hear students express perceptive views about higher education in Canada. In adopting this research strategy, we are following the lead of many other observers of higher education in North America. The major books on universities invariably rest on careful reading, long observation of universities in action, and personal experience within universities.

We occasionally construct hypothetical cases of events and problems at Canadian universities. We do this to provide insight into the intricacies of university politics and decision making. The cases are constructed to give a "hands on" feel for some of the issues and to communicate the rhythms, routines, and patterns of professorial life to readers outside the university.

A number of controversial topics are given short shrift in this book. These include debates about the impact of political correctness on Canadian campuses, controversies about appropriate levels of tuition, and arguments about whether admission requirements should be made more demanding. Such issues are important and merit debate. In our opinion, they are secondary in importance to, and derivative of, the relationships between teaching and research.

This book makes no overt contribution to ongoing debates about public policy toward universities or to broader ideological debates about the role of education. In this regard, we anticipate that some of our thoughts will be borrowed liberally by various hardline critics of universities. But potential borrowers should be cautious. Some conservatives might take our comments about research and teaching and use them to justify further cutbacks to university funding and independence. Such an interpretation would be unwarranted. We exhibit no sympathy for conservative educational views. We are sceptical about markets, certain forms of university-business partnerships, and the use of universities for vocational training. Nor do we share conservative hostility toward affirmative action, feminist ideology, or political correctness. We endorse neither a great-books curriculum nor a back-to-basics educational philosophy. At the end of the day, many of our proposals – for campuses that are more student-friendly, for a redefinition of research and research priorities, for significantly improved teaching – will cause higher education to be much more expensive than at present. They cannot be easily used by anti-university forces.

By the same token, those on the left might see some of our arguments about corporate influence as supportive of their views. But to restate, we see universities as autonomous, independent actors who exercise choice. In our view, they cannot be portrayed as instruments of capitalist rule. Moreover, many readers on the left are unlikely to support some of our views about university priorities in the sphere of teaching. Many left-leaning analyses of universities, while deeply concerned about business power on campus, say little about other basic reforms.

Another general point merits attention. Upon reflection, it is remarkable

how, through the deficit-ridden 1990s, universities internalized the view
that democratic governments have reduced their financial support for
higher education apparently forever. Indeed, a pervasive theme in higher
education policy making is the search for alternative funding. The key
proposition is that universities face ever-increasing costs and declining
government support. As a basic priority they must therefore fund their
operations by finding money elsewhere. But in postdeficit Canada, is it
obvious that governments have forsaken higher education? Is it not possible that higher education will receive better funding from governments,
thereby allowing universities to strengthen teaching and to advance a more
wholesome view of research?

THE ORGANIZATION OF THE BOOK

Chapter 2 examines the development of Canadian universities. It notes
how they are an amalgam of American, English, German, and Scottish influences. It probes the expansion of Canadian universities in the twentieth
century, the growth of research and graduate studies in the 1960s, and the
rise of science and medicine as university powerhouses. Chapter 3 provides
a detailed hypothetical account of a typical academic career in Canada. It
conveys a sense of the obligations and concerns of tenured faculty members. It tries to provide a feel for day-to-day life in a Canadian university
from the vantage point of a professor. It highlights university routines,
professorial priorities, and key steps in a professor's career.

Chapter 4 probes the poor state of undergraduate teaching at Canadian
universities. It argues that teaching is the university's preeminent role. It
then establishes elements of good teaching and shows why good teaching
cannot be achieved without major changes. Chapter 5 examines research
on Canadian campuses. It notes how research plays a major role in all disciplines, in all Canadian universities, and for all professors regardless of their
ideological convictions, political views, or intellectual orientations. It criticizes universities for allowing a very narrow vision of research to dominate.
The chapter points to major discrepancies between ideals of university
research and university research as presently practised in Canada. Chapter 6
examines the interplay between teaching and research. It focuses on the
report of the Commission of Inquiry on Canadian University Education

(hereafter cited as the Smith Report). Authored by Stuart Smith, former leader of the Liberal Party of Ontario, and commissioned by the Association of Universities and Colleges of Canada, the Smith Report shocked Canadian universities by challenging established wisdom about teaching and research.[8] Smith challenged university assertions that teaching is improved when it is undertaken by professors who are active researchers.

Chapter 7 examines ethics in Canadian universities. It argues that competitive universities sometimes breed misconduct and secrecy. Chapter 8 examines the view that universities must link themselves with businesses in the development of profitable goods and services. It reviews university fundraising, advertising, and management practices. It also examines industry-sponsored research. Chapter 8 considers the impact of research partnerships on the quality of teaching and universities' capacity to remain sites of independent analysis.

Chapter 9 reviews conventional wisdom about university reform. It challenges common claims that universities will be much improved by the further application of computer technology, by the removal of tenure, and by the wider introduction of market forces into their operations. We also dissect assertions that Canada would benefit greatly from the development of one or more "world class" research universities. Chapter 10 advances some solutions. Among other things, it calls for rigorous enforcement of university claims that teaching is equal to research as a priority and for more exacting assessment of the quality of research.

CHAPTER 2

THE CANADIAN UNIVERSITY

From College to Knowledge Factory

A century ago, Canada had a handful of colleges and universities with modest enrolments. Higher education was then struggling to define itself in relation to government, organized religion, and the broader society. Fifty years ago, Canadian universities were still unassuming institutions with small enrolments, limited research activity, and narrow ambitions. Their emergence as economic and political powerhouses is an interesting and important story.

This chapter reviews the growth of university education in Canada. It notes that universities have steadily expanded the scope of their activities and assumed many new roles. The result of this expansion of functions and ambition is the "multiversity," a complex and powerful institution that embraces several quite different educational philosophies within its walls.

No single philosophy, public policy, or dominant personality has decisively shaped Canadian higher education. On the contrary, Canadian universities have been influenced by the practices and philosophy of higher education in England, Germany, Scotland, and the United States. They have also been shaped by changing democratic ideals, by the imperatives of an expanding economy, and by the forces of bureaucracy and urbanization.

Since the end of the Second World War, American ideals, practices, and personnel have dominated Canadian universities. Large American universities, with their emphasis on research by tenured faculty, with their commitment to world-class researchers within their ranks, and with their stress on advanced scientific and medical research have become the models for Canadian universities. The chapter pays particular attention to the spectacular expansion of Canadian universities in the 1960s, as this was a decisive decade.

We examine several basic characteristics of Canadian universities in the early twenty-first century. The chapter explores the growth of a professional administrative class within universities, almost identical university "visions" notwithstanding major differences in size, history, and geographical location, and most importantly, the emergence of professorial power and a commitment to research as a fundamental university priority.

This chapter is not a comprehensive history of higher education in Canada. It simply outlines main trends and important changes. Readers in search of more detailed accounts are referred to several excellent works on the subject.[1] We do not canvass the development of particular universities, although we make frequent reference to the University of Toronto, which has been very influential.

While universities are primarily the constitutional responsibility of the provincial governments, we do not compare provincial systems of higher education. Instead, we examine those common characteristics of Canadian universities that, early in the twenty-first century, transcend their different histories, unique cultures, and geographical locations. We are impressed by the similarity of modern Canadian universities despite the very different political and ideological climates that spawned them. The University of Quebec, a product of modern Quebec nationalism; Dalhousie University in Halifax, a product of nineteenth-century religious rivalries in Nova Scotia; and the University of Alberta, the product of a rugged, sparsely populated "new" society are now philosophically and operationally identical. Such remarkable likeness reflects the homogenizing impact of American research universities and the homogenizing impact of specialized academic disciplines that dominate North American universities.

CANADIAN UNIVERSITIES: INTERNATIONAL INFLUENCES

Canadian universities have been shaped by the philosophies of England's two great universities: Oxford and Cambridge. In those universities during the nineteenth century, a distinctive, much revered educational tradition developed. In the classic English model, knowledge, a deeper understanding of the human condition, was sought as an end in itself. Research, as now understood, was not a university priority. Through teaching, the university transmitted humanity's store of knowledge. Professors were charged with the task of careful reflection about the human condition. Curriculum stressed history, classical languages (notably Greek and Latin), and philosophy. Science, as now understood, was not a priority.

Oxford and Cambridge were closely linked to the Church of England. But their studies, while influenced by Christian ideals, were neither narrow nor dogmatic. The Oxbridge mission was to educate elites and to build character and leadership. As Louis-Philippe Bonneau and J.A. Corry put it: "The duty of the university was to prepare an elite not so much for piety as for power and leadership in Church and State. For this purpose, it nearly sufficed to inculcate the high English culture."[2]

Oxford and Cambridge exerted a powerful impact on Canadians' thinking about higher education in an important, practical way. Oxford and Cambridge were the prime source of faculty members for Canadian universities until well into the twentieth century. To use today's language, they were the universities "of choice" for talented Canadians.

At a deeper level, the grand Oxbridge tradition provides a powerful and enduring vision of what a university *should* be. Even today, the nineteenth-century English university symbolizes a safe haven, a refuge from the bustle and materialism of modern civilization. The university in this sense is "a sanctuary of scholarship."[3] The Oxbridge vision sees universities as deeply committed to teaching and to enriching society in noneconomic ways. It remains the inspiration for those who see the humanities, literature, and philosophy as the cornerstone of human civilization.

High-minded English ideals were influential but not dominant in Canada and the United States. Both countries were rough, new societies bent on territorial expansion, economic growth, and the establishment of political orders different from Europe. The serene life of an Oxford college was not easily replicated on their soil. Other philosophies and customs, notably the ways of Scotland's great universities, were influential in North America.

In the nineteenth century, the University of Edinburgh was very different from the great English universities.[4] Its curriculum was more practical.

Research was viewed as an acceptable university undertaking, and science – natural philosophy as it was then called – was important. Edinburgh was independent of the Church of Scotland and more egalitarian than its English counterparts. Able students, regardless of social standing or wealth, attended and were aided by scholarships. Scottish universities had a work ethic, a sense that intellectual life was a demanding one that required perseverance and self-discipline. The university, far from being a haven, was part of a bustling commercial culture. Its lectures were attended by a cross-section of the society. Scottish ideals were influential in the development of three major Canadian universities: Dalhousie, McGill, and Queen's. They are robust antidotes to the gentler English tradition.

Canadian universities were also shaped by American developments in the nineteenth and twentieth centuries. In the United States, Congress passed the Morrill Act in 1862, which provided for the transfer of public lands to educational institutions. In this way, an impressive system of public universities was created in many American states.

Land grant universities are distinctively American institutions. In contrast to Oxford and Cambridge, they were dedicated to the practical needs of an expanding country. Their strengths were agriculture, business management, and engineering, subjects that had no home in European universities. They were public universities created by governments and independent of religious influence.

Land grant universities, which have become such renowned places as the University of Michigan and the University of Wisconsin, were inspired by democratic ideals. They were dedicated to teaching large numbers of students and charged with doing practical research. Their admissions policies were based on merit not social standing.

Land grant universities undertook innovative policies of outreach to communities. Their agricultural departments became forces in the development of American agriculture. Professors were common sights in the cornfields and in the barn as they worked with farmers on disease control and crop development. Clark Kerr has succinctly summarized the impact of the land grant movement in the following terms: "It created a new social force in human history. Nowhere before had universities been so closely linked with the daily life of so much of their societies. The university campus came to be one of the most heavily travelled crossroads in America –

an intersection traversed by farmers, businessmen, politicians, students from almost every corner of almost every state."[5]

Land grant ideals shaped the universities of Alberta, British Columbia, and Saskatchewan. These universities, in Canada's three most westerly provinces, grew up in physical proximity to American land grant universities and were inspired by American thinking. Like land grant universities, they were conceived as public institutions, unlike universities in the Maritimes, Quebec, and Ontario, which grew up under the influence of the Anglican, Baptist, Methodist, Presbyterian, and Roman Catholic Churches.

The land grant legacy is important in other ways. Its ideals formed the intellectual foundation for the tremendous postwar expansion of enrolment in Canadian universities. Canadian governments' controversial goal in the 1960s – that qualified applications should find a place at a Canadian university – is a modern variation of a land grant principle. Land grant ideals also provide an intellectual base for those who see the university's role as serving national economic priorities. It offers a vision of higher education that sees the university, to again use today's parlance, as a partner of society.

A new conception of universities emerged in nineteenth-century Germany. The major German universities, notably the University of Berlin, saw scientific research as the essence of university life. In German universities, the teaching of undergraduate students, a defining characteristic of English, Scottish, and American universities, was secondary to specialized research. To the extent that teaching was significant in Germany, it was related to graduate studies, which culminated in the advanced Doctor of Philosophy degree. The PhD was awarded for the successful completion of a piece of original, specialized research under the guidance of a professor. The German university established a powerful link between high-quality university research and national economic prowess. In George Dennis O'Brien's words: "The development of advanced technological industry (chemistry in particular) in Germany demonstrated the power of research in creating new products. The university, instead of being a removed religious refuge, became an engine of economic advance."[6]

The nineteenth-century German university established two significant new ideas in higher education: that professors were researchers, and that advanced scientific research was central to a great university. In the United States, a radical departure occurred with the creation of the Johns Hopkins

University in Baltimore. Johns Hopkins was an American replica of the University of Berlin that was dedicated to scientific and medical research and graduate studies. Early in the twentieth century, the philosophy of Johns Hopkins University made its presence known at University of Toronto and McGill. While heavily contested in Canada, the German model grew in prestige, especially among university-based scientists, who began to define research as their mission.

The German university has an even deeper influence. It embodied an idea, revolutionary to human civilization, that knowledge was something that could be "produced" at a university. And if knowledge can be produced, it required, just like automobiles or furniture, an underpinning organization and division of labour. Henceforth, university life became specialized. The intellectual world was carved into departments – history, biology, civil engineering, and physics to name just a few – that housed experts in each field of study. Early in the twentieth century, university professors in Canada became organized into ranks, a development that made universities similar to other large organizations. The new faculty member was hired as an assistant professor who, upon satisfactory performance, was promoted to associate professor, and then, subject to distinguished accomplishments, to the rank of professor. These trends are explored in greater detail in Chapter 3, which probes the career and day-to-day activities of a fictitious Canadian professor.

THE EDUCATION OF PROFESSIONALS

Modern Canadian universities educate potential members of professions such as law, medicine, dentistry, and veterinary science. Indeed, it is now a given for Canadians that practitioners of such important occupations require specialized education, that the university is the proper site for such schooling, and that an advanced university degree is a requirement for professional practice. Canadian universities now monopolize education for established professions and for nursing, occupational therapy, forestry, and school teaching. However, the formal affiliation of professions and universities is a relatively new development in higher education.

Throughout the nineteenth century and well into the twentieth, controversy raged about the best way to educate professionals. Debate centred on two questions – what must professionals know? and where and how should they learn?[7] In Canada, legal education outside Quebec followed the British tradition, which stressed apprenticeship in a law firm. As law became more complex, more attention was paid to book learning. But courses were generally offered by provincial law societies not universities. It was not until after the Second World War that the present model of legal education – a three-year university program in law following at least two years of university study, followed by a brief apprenticeship in a law firm and the successful completion of provincial bar examinations – became the Canadian norm.

The development of close links between organized medicine and universities in North America is an important story. Before the twentieth century, North American universities occasionally had medical schools. For example, Benjamin Franklin was adamant that the fledgling University of Pennsylvania must offer formal medical education. But physicians were not obliged to study at universities, let alone earn a degree. "Medical schools were long merely groups of local practitioners, nominally, if at all, associated with universities."[8] Throughout the nineteenth century, the regulation of medical practice by government was minimal, the concept of medical science was not widely understood, and the large general hospital was only emerging as the locus of medical care in cities. Compared with the twentieth century, the overall quality of medical care was poor.

In 1910, Abraham Flexner, an ardent admirer of German research universities, was commissioned by the Carnegie Foundation to examine the state of medical education in North America. His landmark report documented inferior facilities, weak faculty, and inadequate curriculum (although the University of Toronto and McGill University were ranked among the ten best medical schools in North America). His report led to what is now called "a rationalization" of medical education. Many medical schools were closed and those that remained were substantially reformed.

A new model of medical education emerged. Johns Hopkins University, following the model of the University of Edinburgh, was again the pioneer. It established a medical faculty and affiliated it with a substantial university hospital. In the Edinburgh and Hopkins' view, medicine was a major field of scientific study and an area of advanced graduate work. Medical students were expected to have undertaken serious prior study in natural science, mathematics, and philosophy. Medicine was also to be underpinned by advanced research, a cause that was given worldwide impetus by the discovery of insulin by university-based Canadian medical scientists. In a very short period, a revolution had occurred. As A.B. McKillop puts it, "From the surgery of the gentleman practitioner, the locus of medicine's authority had shifted first to the hospital wards and later into hospital and university laboratories."[9]

The transformation of medical education into a university-based science yielded substantial advances in standards of treatment, in the overall quality of health care, and, through research, into a deeper understanding of illness. Canadian universities were transformed by these developments. The advent of large medical faculties allied with major hospitals added complexity to universities. Modern medical science is expensive and can strain university resources. The medical faculty, through its prestige, through its link with physicians in communities, and through its high status in the eyes of governments, became a potent force in university priority setting. Major research universities came to see advanced medical science as their forte.[10] The career mobility of successful medical scientists, their high standing in society, and their large salaries made them both feared and envied in universities. Such envy and fear is heightened by the limited links between medicine and other parts of the university and by the simple fact that university hospitals are sometimes physically distant from the main university campus. For these reasons, medical scientists and Faculties of Medicine remain mysterious sources of great reputed power.

By the 1960s, the foundations of the modern Canadian university had been built. The university, like its American counterpart, embraced three distinct, often conflicting dimensions: large undergraduate programs in arts and science; professional faculties, notably medicine, law, and engineering, where students are trained for occupations; and graduate faculties, where faculty undertook research and students pursued advanced degrees. Readers will legitimately ask, why are these very different activities not housed in separate institutions?

No distinctively Canadian ideas have emerged about the role of the university, the deeper purposes of higher education, or intellectual life in general. The dominant influence of other metropolitan centres is obvious. Oxbridge ideals about higher education as transmission of culture and character building combined with practical Scottish ideals provided a foundation for undergraduate teaching as the main task of universities. The German influence manifests itself in an emphasis on rigorous graduate studies and advanced scientific research. In the German tradition, the professor was primarily a researcher not a teacher. The University of Toronto and McGill were early outposts of this notion. The egalitarian and public service impulses of the great public universities in Wisconsin, Michigan, Texas, and Ohio provided examples of close relations between universities, business and society, applied research, and practical programs of study.

In the 1950s, Canadian universities were still relatively modest institutions. The University of Toronto was a dominant force and Canada's only player in the major leagues of North American universities. Its governance structure, with a board of trustees responsible for the financial affairs and general policy of the university and a senate of professors who dealt with curriculum matters, became the norm. Toronto had been an early advocate of research ideals. But even at Toronto, British influences remained strong, many professors continued to define themselves as teachers, and undergraduate studies were significant. As late as the 1960s, the influence of organized religion was still felt from time to time throughout the country.[11]

Canadian universities were linked with business through their Faculties of Engineering and Commerce. New fields of study were emerging. Carleton College in Ottawa, soon to be Carleton University, was established in 1948 to educate Second World War veterans. But at this time, Canadian universities harboured no grand visions. They were still poorly funded and operated without stable government support. They were still small enough to be dominated, or at least heavily influenced, by their presidents. It was in the 1960s that Canadian universities assumed major new roles and greater public prominence. An "academic revolution" took place.

THE ACADEMIC REVOLUTION IN CANADA

The 1960s were a period of unprecedented expansion and substantial change in Canadian universities. The number of students enrolled grew substantially. Women were admitted in record numbers and began to make their presence felt in law and engineering, to name just a few areas. New universities were created throughout Canada. These included York

University in suburban Toronto; Simon Fraser University in Burnaby, British Columbia; the University of Lethbridge in Lethbridge, Alberta; and Brock University, Laurentian University, Lakehead University, and Trent University in St. Catharines, Sudbury, Thunder Bay, and Peterborough, Ontario, respectively.

Another development was the amalgamation of colleges into public universities. Witness the University of Prince Edward Island, formed through the merger of Prince of Wales College and St. Dunstan's University, and Concordia University in Montreal, formed through the merger of Sir George Williams University and Loyola College. In Quebec, an entirely new university system, University of Quebec, was established. The main campus was in Montreal, with satellites in smaller communities such as Trois Rivières and Chicoutimi.

Throughout Canada, new programs were created and existing ones expanded. Previously underdeveloped fields like sociology and anthropology became major sources of enrolment. Graduate studies and research, long the second fiddles to undergraduate programs in arts and science, assumed greater significance. Universities without advanced degrees soon considered themselves inferior and moved into the graduate field. Professors were required to design new programs of research and to supervise students in the burgeoning graduate faculties. Higher education was seen as a positive force in terms of economic development and personal development. Its North American expansion, while significant, was essentially unplanned and conducted without an overarching vision or sense of priorities.

Two forces explain the substantial postwar growth of universities in Canada and the United States. First, science and scientific research assumed enormous importance throughout the democratic world, especially in the United States. The Second World War saw an impressive expansion of scientific endeavour and achievement, particularly in the United States. America's military and industrial prowess was fuelled by scientific and research capacity. Governments in the United States launched major national programs of research in defence-related areas, health, and general science. To an unprecedented degree, America's universities became wedded to the federal government and to the pursuit of complex scientific research in the national interest. As *The Economist* puts it, "Scientific investigation has become the key function of the modern research university, the well spring of its confidence – almost, in the minds of many of its employees, its raison d'être."[12]

A second impressive force was the rapid growth of demand for university education in North America. By the mid-1960s, baby boomers were moving through high school toward universities in large numbers. In this environment and in a prosperous era, higher education became, if not an entitlement, something that would be experienced by most middle-class Canadians. Access to university education quickly became associated with good jobs, a high standard of living, and excellent life prospects. Some observers lamented that university education, if seen as a citizen right, would deteriorate in quality to soon resemble a glorified high school education.[13] In the heady 1960s, these were voices in the wilderness that were dismissed as inevitable reactions to rapid change.

In the 1960s, Canadian universities became closely linked with governments. The Government of Canada and the provincial governments became deeply involved in university activities, although for different reasons and in different ways. Governments shared the general societal enthusiasm for university education. Stripped bare, their position was simple – decent public universities with open admission policies were good politics and a major investment in economic development. A well-educated workforce was a productive one, and an expanding industrial economy required a solid research base.

The Government of Canada became committed to the support of university research in science, engineering, medicine, and, to a lesser degree, arts, social sciences, and humanities. This role was compatible with its broader interests in national economic development and, given aggressive Quebec nationalism, the view that higher education was a provincial prerogative. For their part, the provinces funded the construction and subsequent operation of an expanding roster of provincial universities. This role was complex and caused the creation of major provincial government departments charged with the development of university funding and admissions policies. In essence, the provinces funded teaching while Ottawa paid the direct costs of an expanding university research program.

The upshot of these trends was what J.A. Corry calls the transformation of the Canadian university into a "public utility."[14] The university, for decades a private institution with limited public purposes, became a public body linked with governments. Government funding provided Canadian universities with financial stability. It also guaranteed that the academy's priorities would be shaped by democratic politics and economic needs.

The 1960s also witnessed the emergence of the American research university as the ideal to which Canadian universities aspired. British influences waned as faculty were recruited in great numbers from American graduate schools. Undergraduate programs and teaching began to take a back seat to graduate studies and research as university priorities. A new vision of the professor also emerged. She was to be a researcher, a director of advanced research by graduate students, and an undergraduate teacher. This new definition of the professor permeated the university. It was embraced by engineers, botanists, historians, and even philosophers. When challenged by critics, advocates of research found a clever way to wish away a clash of priorities between research and undergraduate students. Everybody knew, didn't they, that in American universities, faculty research inspired the classroom. Active researchers allegedly brought energy and new insight into their teaching in ways that nonresearchers could not replicate. Everyone also knew that good teachers were good researchers. A powerful new idea had emerged.

THE CANADIAN MULTIVERSITY IN ACTION

In the 1960s, Canadian universities began to take the shape of "multiversities." Within universities there emerged three quite distinct universities – professional schools, especially medicine; the large Faculties of Arts and Science, which taught most of the students; and the graduate programs where research was the focus. Several characteristics of the new Canadian university are particularly distinctive and are explored here. Some of the characteristics are structural while others describe a state of mind, the culture of the university.

The Emergence of a University System
The growing influence of public policy on universities led to new forms of interaction as governments tried to shape university priorities and hold them accountable. In the provinces, concerns mounted about program

"duplication"; the need for common standards for admission; and links between universities, the growing system of community colleges, and high schools. A structure of coordinating committees emerged.

Similar processes occurred nationally. Universities, while nominally provincial institutions, became linked with the Government of Canada. National pressure groups for the universities, the Association of Universities and Colleges of Canada (AUCC), and for university professors, the Canadian Association of University Professors (CAUT), grew in importance.

While universities sometimes compete for public recognition and resources, they also share important common interests. For AUCC, the objective is increased research funding, while CAUT wants common national employment standards and greater public recognition for professors.

Universities now make up a major national interest group. Like business, agriculture, and organized labour, they have common policy interests and operate as national, not simply provincial, institutions.

Common Visions
As the twentieth century progressed, Canadian universities became increasingly similar in their organization and sense of purpose. In the nineteenth and early twentieth century, universities were quite different from each other. Many were shaped by organized religions, which demanded that they differ. In a simpler Canada, universities remained parts of local milieus. They were themselves simpler institutions dedicated primarily to teaching and linked loosely to major European and American universities.

As research became more important and as American ideals dominated, universities assumed a common veneer. Each now wants to be recognized for the quality of its researchers, each wants to recruit superior faculty and students, and each wants to be relevant to the broader society. Universities now claim that they can develop technologically advanced products and processes.

When occasionally challenged about this uniformity of priorities, universities respond that they really cannot be different. If they strike a distinctive course, they may not be able to recruit the best faculty and students. These would flock to the other universities that embody the mainstream ideals of faculty research and graduate studies. A vicious circle had obviously been created.

The Growth of University Bureaucracy

For outsiders, the university is an elaborate organization whose operating principles are cumbersome. Business leaders often mock universities as committee-dominated mazes where decision making is painfully slow, often petty, and far too democratic for their tastes and experiences. No one seems to be in command. This view of university decision making has gained notoriety throughout society and is reflected in novels and mass media. The popular idea is captured by the remark, knowingly expressed by outsiders to universities, that the intensity of university debate is inversely related to the significance of the issue.

Such views about university decision making are not myth, but they are incomplete. The image of university as organized anarchy describes the activities of professors when they are deciding matters such as curriculum, admissions standards, and their own evaluations. It omits a much broader development in twentieth-century society – the emergence of university bureaucracy. In this sense, universities, far from being exotic and mysterious, are treading the well-worn path of corporations, governments, and hospitals.

Each university has a civil service consisting of full-time, nonteaching staff to do three principal things: handle student admissions and records, manage and promote the university's scientific and medical research programs, and manage the personnel commitments of large universities, which employ thousands of staff and which are major employers in many Canadian cities. Such activities are undertaken in a manner remarkably similar to other large organizations.

Universities now have administrative elites. Until recently, university presidents were major intellectual forces. They were accomplished scholars who exercised detailed control over their campuses. Lesser officers of the university – deans of faculties, heads of departments, and even vice-presidents – were part-timers who continued serious scholarly careers.

University administration is now a demanding, full-time job. Academic leaders, with the exception of those at the lowest level, department heads, normally pursue careers in academic administration. They sometimes aspire to rise through the university hierarchy. As a result, they sometimes become far removed from teaching and serious scholarship. Professional administrators are required for activities such as public relations, fund-raising, and computer systems. University librarians, once the custodians of books and documents, now sport titles such as director of learning services or vice-president for information technology. The administration of research grants consumes a large office in every university.

The growth of university administration has major consequences. It is a source of faculty grievance even though most of it promotes research and the university's image, activities highly sought after by professors. More-over, professional university administrators add a new element to universities' power structure. Senior administrators interpret the university to society at large, explain its priorities, and justify its behaviour. Professional administrators have an even stronger interest in the prestige of the university than do faculty members. Finally, the growth of university administration has made university management a career option for people who are professional managers and who have no emotional ties to, or particular interest in, universities. Canadian universities are now linked through their managers to corporations, government bureaucracies, and community colleges. This factor partially explains the widely noted adoption by universities of the style and rhetoric of corporate management, including references to students as "clients" or even "customers."

Modern Professors
University teaching and research are now very specialized. Professors seldom have broad expertise. On the contrary, they are experts in specialized areas. Academic life has a complex division of labour.

In this environment, university departments have little contact with each other. The Department of Economics, for example, has few links with the Departments of Political Science and Sociology, let alone the Departments of Accounting, Physics, or Corporate Law. A theoretical economist may have more in common with a mathematician than with another economist who is expert in the banking industry. Each discipline is in charge of its own affairs. In Canadian universities, botanists hire other botanists, English professors evaluate English professors, and biochemists assess the research of other biochemists. A fundamental belief is that members of one discipline cannot really judge, teach, or do research in other disciplines. The modern university is a federation loosely linked by a broad interest in learning and research but with little else in common.

Specialization and a highly developed division of labour characterize and mould universities. The professor is now best described as a knowledge worker who pursues narrow research in a highly structured university and who relates primarily to comparable specialists. Far from being an intimidating figure full of wisdom about the human condition, the modern professor is a generally an expert on a specific subject.

The modern professoriate is a complex occupational group. At its pinnacle is the tenured professor at a major university. But underpinning her and, as we shall see, serving her interests, are lesser paid, lower status instructors. Such staff have different titles at different universities, including "sessional lecturers," "visiting professors," or "term appointments." Regardless of title, their role and lot is broadly similar. They have positions limited to a specified period, often of one year. They have no sense of permanence or security. They often teach large, demanding classes of first- and second-year students. They enjoy neither the same salaries as tenured professors nor the same benefits. They seldom have much influence in university policy making.

Temporary professors aspire to tenured status, but positions were very hard to come by in the 1980s and 1990s. Moreover, competition remains stiff and heavily based on research accomplishments. The sessional staff frequently move to assume sessional positions at other universities when their contracts expire. They feel (justifiably) exploited by a system in which they are lowly members.

Injustice in the University

A Canadian university president of a century ago would be astounded by a return to campus in the third millennium. He would be particularly surprised by the massive increase in enrolment, the depth of professorial commitment to research, and the spectacular growth of laboratories and science buildings. The returning president would also be amazed by the overall quality of buildings and teaching facilities, which are now luxurious compared to 50, let alone 100, years ago. He would be astonished by the rhetoric of today's presidents that claims, primarily for economic reasons, that universities are society's most valuable institutions, treasure troves of research excellence that are national assets. The pervasive sense of injustice in the university would be especially noteworthy to the time traveller.

No modern institution is so rife with jealousy and a sense of oppression as the modern university. The lines of conflict are innumerable. Sessional staff resent tenured professors, whom they see as pampered and self-serving. Professors in arts feel undervalued compared with every one else. They resentfully see themselves as second fiddles to medical professors and natural scientists, who get the limelight and public acclaim. Some professors resent their colleagues who undertake administrative work. Dedicated teachers often despise researchers who ignore their students with impunity. Accomplished researchers sometimes return the favour by calling skilled teachers "deadwood." Most professors believe every other university is a better employer, one that provides more money for research, travel, and books and that wisely demands less teaching. Most professors believe that other universities have better presidents, ones who understand the faculty members and deal more effectively with governments. Female professors claim overt and subtle discrimination by male colleagues. The list goes on and on.

Universities now see themselves as institutions whose underfunding threatens national well-being. Moreover, modern professors – well-paid, highly respected in society, free to pursue their own agendas – are often full of grievances. Many professors see the university as surrounded by critical governments and a society that misunderstands and undervalues research. Life in Canadian universities is stressful, often unhappy, and sometimes conflict-ridden.

CONCLUSION

Canadian universities grew impressively in the twentieth century. The growth was topsy-turvy and without the guidance of a master plan. The basic purposes of higher education remain in dispute. An enduring controversy is whether universities, as amalgams of professional, undergraduate, and research programs, pursue too many competing ends and house too many contradictory visions. In the eyes of some critics, higher education does too many things, none very well. By the same token, does university research justify the resources expended on it? Do universities teach the "right" things? Might some university research be better undertaken by nonuniversity organizations? Can universities really develop goods and services for the economy?

Before exploring these questions, we want to give readers a better sense of Canadian universities by outlining a typical academic career. We try to show the routines of university life, the roles of key players, and the often complicated duties of a professor.

CHAPTER 3

UNIVERSITIES IN ACTION

A Day in the Life

This chapter sketches the career and day-to-day activities of a fictitious Canadian professor. It tries to give nonacademic readers a sense of the rhythms, tedium, and dynamics of modern university life. Our fictitious professor, Dr. Wayne Young, is typical in the sense that the central features of both his career as a whole and his daily regimen are normal rather than exceptional for Canadian academics. However, Professor Young is not typical in the sense that he is (for example) "average" based on a sample survey of Canadian psychology professors. He is an invention, albeit based on our reading, formal interviews, numerous casual conversations with psychologists and other professors, and our several decades as academic social scientists.

This chapter highlights several important features of Canadian universities that we discuss in this book. Two key points, universities' emphasis on research and the power of tenured professors, are stressed.

THE BIOGRAPHY

Dr. Wayne Young is professor of psychology at McMaster University in Hamilton, Ontario. Born in 1950 and raised in a middle-class suburb of Toronto, Wayne was a gifted student in high school. He entered York University in 1968, intending to major in psychology because, as he said, he "wanted to find out what makes people tick." At that time, he thought that academic psychology probed large, complex questions about the human condition.

While at York, Wayne quickly learned that most academic psychology is not about deeper questions of human behaviour. For example, university psychologists don't often study major questions such as, Why are some people shy and others outgoing? Why are some people afraid of heights and others of enclosed spaces? Are men naturally more aggressive than women? Is there a maternal instinct? The studies pursued by most university psychologists are similar to those that interest biologists, physiologists, and neurologists. They are precise investigations of specific topics undertaken principally through the device of carefully conceived laboratory experiments. For this reason, most university Departments of Psychology are located in Faculties of Science, along with physics and biology, rather than in Faculties of Arts, along with sociology, literature, and history. (Some psychology departments are in both Faculties of Science and Faculties of Arts.)

Wayne became fascinated with academic psychology. He excelled at it. As a result, he was invited to become an honours student, a status that enabled him to concentrate quite heavily on psychology during the last two of his four years as an undergraduate. He was especially pleased to be able to work in the laboratory of one of York's distinguished psychologists in the summer of his final year as an undergraduate. Some of his friends began to call him "Rat-boy," because his lab work involved careful observation of the reaction of laboratory rats to sounds. He took the ribbing with good humour because he loved the work.

Wayne completed his bachelor of arts at York and then entered the master's program in psychology at the University of Toronto, where he also excelled. A distinguished professor of psychology took an interest in him and actively encouraged him to pursue an academic career. By this time he required little encouragement. The professor urged him to apply to the PhD programs of the best American universities for three reasons. First, he would receive the best education possible there. Second, only that kind of degree would guarantee him an eventual position at a top university, either in the United States or in Canada. In other words, major American universities are seen as prestigious. Its graduates are assumed to be good and thus are sought after. Prestige and reputation are matters central to scholarly life. Third, a major American university was likely to provide better scholarship assistance than a Canadian university. Wayne was counselled to apply widely at American universities and then assess the offers bearing in mind the paramount need to study at a university of considerable reputation.

Wayne completed his master's thesis in the summer of 1974. Several major American universities offered him positions in their PhD programs, with financial assistance that would keep the wolf far from his door. He finally accepted the offer from Yale, mainly because he wanted to work with the famous student of animal behaviour, Professor John J. Stevens.

J.J. Stevens was widely renowned for his pioneering research on the effect of various foods and drugs on the vision of rats. Most academic psychology is quite distant from everyday life. Stevens' work actually held potential significance for matters of human importance. Stevens was especially interested in the effects of alcohol on the vision of rats. There was a real possibility that his work would make a significant contribution to the understanding of alcoholism and other kinds of drug abuse. Stevens was sometimes consulted by governments and by distillers and brewers that had an interest in his work. Wayne was thrilled when a "superstar" of J.J. Stevens' stature agreed to supervise his PhD work.

Wayne spent his first year at Yale taking advanced courses in psychological theory and methods of research. In addition, he was paid $25,000 per year (as well as having his fees waived) to act as Professor Stevens' research assistant. In that capacity, Wayne was expected to work for twelve hours a week but he usually did twenty. He performed various tasks for Stevens, including photocopying and tracking down scientific papers from the library. He also assisted in Stevens' undergraduate courses. With little guidance and with no background training or preparation, he began to supervise undergraduates in labs and to mark their lab reports. During his second year in the PhD program, Wayne began to do more complex work in the lab. He also began to do specialized reading in academic periodicals. He concentrated on reports of new research on the effects of diet on the vision of rats. In addition, he was by now spending about ten hours a day in the lab, seven days a week.

Halfway through this second year Wayne faced the first major hurdle of the PhD student: he took his comprehensive examinations, or "comps" as they are known. A PhD student must pass comprehensive examinations before beginning intensive work on the PhD thesis. These examinations claim to test students' general understanding of their field, students' special knowledge of their area of specialization, and their near-mastery of the area in which they propose to write a PhD thesis. In Wayne's case, this meant examinations in psychological theory, methodology, animal behaviour, and nutrient-brain interactions. The examinations were set and graded by Wayne's PhD committee, consisting of his supervisor Professor Stevens and four other professors. The members of this committee set and assessed Wayne's written examinations and then questioned him for about two hours during an oral examination. Wayne passed his comprehensive examinations with distinction.

Three aspects of the comprehensive examination process are noteworthy. First, only one member of the examining committee was from an academic discipline other than psychology. A sociologist, the "external examiner," asked a few questions but made no real effort to see whether Wayne grasped larger issues or intellectual traditions. Second, the comps in psychology were the only place where Wayne's general knowledge was probed. But even at this crucial juncture the paramount question was whether Wayne knew a specialized literature well enough to do his thesis. Finally, Wayne's comps, like all others, raised no questions about how students should be *taught* psychology. Wayne was evaluated exclusively as a potential researcher.

After he completed his comprehensive examinations, Wayne began to collaborate more closely with Professor Stevens and his team of associates (an assistant professor, a visiting professor from New Zealand, and two postdoctoral fellowship holders.) Before long, Wayne was listed, along with Professor Stevens and one or more other members of the team, as coauthor of a few academic papers. Stevens often told Wayne that publishing was essential to a successful career and that he must develop a systematic research and publication strategy.

Stevens carefully explained to Wayne how scholarly journals operated in North America. He noted the major, independent role for journal editors who were prominent psychologists with major research records. Moreover, Stevens schooled Wayne in the hierarchy of journals. He explained why some were more important than others and which ones Wayne should try to be published in. He told him about peer review whereby journal editors solicit reviews of manuscripts from other specialists in the area. Peer review is blind, that is, the reviewer is not aware of the author's identity and vice versa. The peer reviewers' judgments are very important in the evaluation of articles and hence careers. Finally, Stevens told Wayne some basic facts of academic life. Academic journals prefer technically competent, narrowly focused research. Their forte is the specific not the general. Manuscripts that assume critical stances, that advocate alternative methodologies, and that challenge conventional truths are seldom accepted unless they are stellar.

During this period, Wayne was preparing to write his PhD thesis. Stated simply, the experiments for his PhD were concerned with the comparison between certain brain activities of rats after they had consumed various amounts of alcohol and cocaine. When Stevens and the other members of his PhD committee were convinced that Wayne had enough positive results, he was allowed to go ahead and write his thesis.

His Yale PhD in hand, Wayne, who wanted to return to Canada, found an excellent position as a postdoctoral fellow at the University of Alberta, where there is a strong Department of Psychology. At Alberta, he was able to work with an eminent student of visual anomalies in animals, Professor Kathleen Johnson. Wayne spent two years in Alberta. During the first year he spent innumerable hours in Dr. Johnson's lab, collaborating with her, in a junior capacity, in her experiments on rats' ability to see in various kinds of light. At the same time he wrote two papers based on his PhD thesis. These papers were published in psychological journals. In both cases, his PhD supervisor, J.J. Stevens, was listed as coauthor, as is the practice in the natural sciences.

During his second year at the University of Alberta, Wayne continued his collaboration with Professor Johnson, publishing three papers as one of her coauthors. He also got his first taste of teaching, offering an introductory course in animal perception to a class of forty third-year psychology majors. Wayne was asked to teach this course because a senior professor received a major research grant that allowed him to opt out of teaching for a year. Wayne was neither mentored nor trained in the complexities of undergraduate teaching. No prior assessment was made of his abilities or temperament and no serious analysis was undertaken of his first major teaching experience.

During Wayne's second year of working with Professor Johnson, the Department of Psychology at McMaster University advertised a potentially permanent job in Wayne's field. (In the jargon of academe, this was a tenure-track position.) Wayne applied along with 150 other people (McMaster is an excellent university and permanent jobs were scarce). Six weeks after his application, he received a letter informing him that he had made the shortlist of three candidates: those who would fly to Hamilton at McMaster's expense for interviews to decide who would be offered the job. Wayne performed well in his interviews. But more important were three facts. First, he had received his PhD from Yale, a prestigious Ivy League university with worldwide reputation. The Yale degree was a major advantage. Second, Stevens at Yale and Johnson at Alberta, highly distinguished psychologists, gave Wayne glowing recommendations. And third, Wayne had coauthored scholarly articles in prestigious psychological periodicals. As a result, McMaster offered him the job. After negotiations about teaching responsibilities, laboratory facilities, and salary, Wayne was appointed assistant professor of psychology at McMaster University beginning 1 July 1979.

During his interviews at McMaster, Wayne was questioned at length about his research strategy. He was seldom asked about his philosophy of teaching. Nor was he required to give a lecture to undergraduate students as evidence of his classroom acumen. Teaching was primarily discussed during salary negotiations. At that point, McMaster made it clear that Wayne's research would not be slowed by demanding teaching assignments. The university feared that exacting teaching responsibilities would make Wayne vulnerable to offers from other universities promising a lighter teaching load.

Normally, teaching responsibilities (the teaching load, as it's called) in the psychology department at McMaster were four courses: usually two in the first term (September to December) and two in the second (January to April). Each course requires that the professor spend three hours a week in the classroom. Ordinarily, then, the science professor spends six hours a week in the classroom during the academic year. She spends the rest of her time preparing for classes, supervising her teaching assistants, grading essays and examinations, supervising graduate students, serving on committees (at the department, faculty, and university level), and, above all, doing research. (Some scientists also consult for business or government. A few even own businesses related to their specialties, in which they work part time, but this is unusual for academic psychologists.) In his first year, Wayne was given a one-course reduction of his teaching load and was not required to serve on any committees. Moreover, his courses were all relatively advanced courses, with relatively low enrolments, in his areas of special expertise. This meant that he didn't have to spend long hours preparing for classes. It also meant that his students were psychology majors, so that he didn't have to cope with students who had little interest in the subject matter of his courses. The purpose of this "course relief" and freedom from administrative responsibilities was to help Wayne meet the demanding publication standards required for tenure.

Until she is granted tenure (or denied it, which is equivalent to being fired), the status of an assistant professor is probationary. She is appointed for an initial term of four years. At the end of this period the head of her department makes a recommendation to a tenure committee (which is constituted in different ways in different universities) either that she be retained for two more years of probation or that she be fired after one more year of service. Almost invariably, the recommendation is that she be retained. In two more years (that is, after six years as an assistant professor) she is considered for tenure (that is, appointment without definite term; a person with tenure can be fired but she doesn't come up for periodic reappointment). Once again, the head of her department makes a recommendation to a tenure committee.

Wayne's tenure committee, like all those struck at Canadian universities, is supposed to make its decision on the basis of two paramount, equally weighted factors: quality of teaching and quality of research. However, research (or more accurately publications) is decisively more important in practice. Teaching needs only to be adequate. It is possible for a barely acceptable teacher to be granted tenure if she publishes extensively. But it is not possible for a brilliant teacher to be granted tenure if she does not publish, no matter how learned she may be. Furthermore, publication is judged entirely, or almost entirely, on the basis of quantity. Except in rare cases, members of science tenure committees know little about the quality

of the publications they judge. A botanist sat on Wayne's tenure committee. He simply assumed that he had no competence to judge Wayne's
research. Interestingly, two of the three representatives of the Department
of Psychology on Wayne's tenure committee, his colleagues, asked very few
questions. They assumed that Wayne's research could be properly evaluated
only by the sole member of the department who worked in the subfield.

During the first three years, Professor Young was author or coauthor of
eight papers published in well-known psychology journals. In addition, he
made presentations at conferences of psychologists. Although he showed
no distinction as a classroom teacher, Wayne was very helpful to some
graduate students working in his field. As a result, the head of his department happily and strongly recommended that his initial four-year probationary appointment be extended for two more years. His recommendation
was accepted unanimously, quickly, and without controversy.

Wayne's superior performance continued in the following year, during
which he coauthored three papers. His department head even contem-
plated presenting Wayne as a special case whose accomplishments merited
early tenure, that is, tenure after four years not six. But the department head
got cold feet, worrying that he might not be able to convince his colleagues
that Wayne was an emerging superstar. Wayne was very disappointed by
this decision. But he continued to publish regularly. Without controversy,
he received tenure and promotion to the rank of associate professor after
six years.

Early in Wayne's career, J.J. Stevens at Yale and other experienced professors taught him that research accomplishments determined the success of
academic careers. His receipt of tenure on the basis of strong research "productivity" proved the wisdom of their counsel. The value of research also
became apparent to Wayne in the area of university merit pay. McMaster,
like most major universities, has a system of merit pay that recognizes,
although seldom defines, outstanding performance. The theory is that
overall performance must embrace teaching and research. But in Wayne's
department, merit pay decisions were made by counting the number and
length of each professor's published articles. The greater the number
achieved, the larger the merit pay award.

As an associate professor, Wayne's activities and responsibilities changed
somewhat, although research continued to dominate his career. He began

to carry time-consuming administrative responsibilities. In the psychology department, he served on the graduate committee, responsible for selecting and funding graduate students and for overseeing the graduate program. After a few years he became the committee's chairperson, which is an onerous and time-consuming job. He also served as a member of the research committee of the Faculty of Science, which was his sole point of contact with the university beyond the Department of Psychology. He did not interact regularly with other scientists and knew only a handful of professors in other disciplines and faculties.

A second change is that he began to apply for, and receive, large research grants from two of the federal government's granting councils. The larger and more frequent grants came from the Natural Science and Engineering Research Council. A couple of smaller grants came from the Medical Research Council (now the Canadian Institutes of Health Research). Applying for grants is a demanding task, requiring care, creativity, and many hours of tedious work filling out forms. (In universities, the ability to write effective research grant applications is known as "grantsmanship.") So Wayne became a kind of academic entrepreneur. Moreover, since grant applications in science almost invariably are made by more than one professor and include a budget item for the employment of technicians and research assistants, Wayne's research began to involve the management of junior associates.

Wayne's success at the granting councils reveals a major influence on Canadian academic life. The councils shape, directly or indirectly, most major aspects of university life. Their policies influence what is studied, by whom, and under what circumstances. The granting councils allow professors like Wayne to use research money to reduce their teaching commitment. In a given year, several of Wayne's courses will be taught by another professor or by a temporary instructor. This practice is called "time release" or "course buyout." In research universities, its very existence encourages professors to apply for grants. Moreover, granting councils now award research funds primarily on the basis of track record, which means that the more a professor publishes in a field, the more he or she is likely to receive federal funds. Professors are loath to embark on new research areas, as the councils favour the tried and true. Major changes in research emphasis cause a decline in "research productivity" and so they seldom occur.

Finally, Wayne had to teach some larger courses. Except for English departments, psychology departments typically have the largest undergraduate enrolments in Canadian universities. Usually about half this enrolment is concentrated in the introductory course. There is a tradition in the psychology department that the introductory course is taught in huge classes. In some American state universities, classes are taught in gigantic lecture theatres containing 1,000 or more students. McMaster University had no such classes, but Wayne did have a class of 250 students. It was thus impossible for him to give individual attention to students. For that purpose, the tutorial and laboratory sessions for his class were taught by graduate teaching assistants (TAs). Also, grading essays and written examinations for such a large group would take up an unacceptable amount of time given the overriding priority of research. Student evaluation in the course was done by machine-scored multiple-choice examinations.

Wayne gave three lectures a week and supervised the TAs. Lecturing to 250 students (or, rather, the 150 who show up to any given class) requires certain skills. Some of the students are taking the course only because they need it to get into medicine or social work. Some are bored because the course is too easy, others because it is too hard. During any given class, some are completing their chemistry lab reports, some are reading newspapers, and many are daydreaming. Under these circumstances, teaching has as much to do with entertainment (edutainment, as it has been called) as with knowledge of the subject matter and the ability to present it in the simple and straightforward manner appropriate for beginning students. Wayne found that he was simply not cut out for this kind of teaching. Naturally serious, somewhat humourless, and dedicated far more to specialized research than general teaching, he simply couldn't put on the show required to keep the attention of the half of the class for whom this was just another course. After his misadventure with the introductory course, Wayne discharged his responsibility for teaching larger classes by teaching regularly the course on statistics for psychologists. Although this was still a large undergraduate course and somewhat impersonal (as in the introductory course, TAs were mainly responsible for the close contact with students), almost all the students were psychology majors, so holding their attention during lectures was less of a problem. The TAs did all the grading. Teaching statistics, a tool that is important for research in all areas of psychology, suited Wayne's interests and personality. He is not an excellent undergraduate teacher or, for that matter, even an average one, but he is adequate as long as the students are motivated and the subject matter is close to his areas of research interest.

Wayne's uninspired teaching in no way impeded his career. His professional life revolved around his research, other psychologists who shared his interests, and the imperatives of gaining research grants. Undergraduate students seldom entered these orbits. Better and innovative ways to teach, to evaluate students, or to inspire them were never the focus of Wayne's discussion with his colleagues. Neither his department head nor the dean of science ever spoke with Wayne about the elements of serious undergraduate teaching.

Deans, who are the chief administrators of faculties, hold a revered spot in the lore of universities. They often appear in novels and movies about universities. A lingering view outside universities is that deans are distinguished scholars who occupy their positions through demonstrated accomplishment. In practice, they are a diverse group. Most are solid researchers and teachers, but few are distinguished in these areas. Some deans have abandoned scholarship, opting to pursue a career in university administration. A successful or well-known dean may parlay her achievements into a vice-presidential position or even a presidency. But not all deans are ambitious in this way. Some are successful department heads who exhibit a penchant for organization and budgets. Others undertake the task late in a career when no younger professor is willing to interrupt her research.

As an associate professor, Wayne continued to fulfil the promise he had shown from the time he was an eager honours student at York. His research grants grew larger and larger. His laboratory grew in size and became better equipped. He was now known internationally for his scrupulously careful work on the effects of cocaine on the perceptual functioning of rats. More and more PhD candidates sought his supervision. He and his associates produced a steady stream of articles in good psychological journals. The articles guaranteed more grants, the grants guaranteed better equipment and more students and associates, they guaranteed more articles, and so on.

At the beginning of his fifth year as associate professor, the head of Wayne's department urged him to apply for promotion to full professor. Promotion to full professor involves an assessment by a promotion committee on the recommendation of the candidate's department head. This assessment involves evaluation of the candidate's teaching, research, administration, and public service. Assessors devote primary emphasis to research. The number and size of the candidate's research grants, as well as the number of articles in learned journals and the prestige ranking of those journals, are basic considerations. The importance of research is powerfully reinforced by another feature of the process of promotion to full professor. The department head's recommendation must be accompanied by written evaluations of the candidate by at least three respected full professors from other universities, who must not be friends of the candidate. Such external referees have no familiarity with the candidate's teaching, administration, or public service. They know him from his publications and from his performance at professional conferences, that is, as a researcher. Under these rules, Wayne was promoted with no hesitation. He was a full professor at the age of thirty-eight, which is unusually young.

As a full professor, Wayne has continued to flourish. The articles, grants, and PhD students seeking his supervision continue to flow. His colleagues hold him in high esteem. In fact, a solid majority favours him as the next head of the department. Wayne finds this flattering, but he is not tempted. Chairing a university department has few rewards and many headaches. (At most universities, the term "chairman" replaced the term "head" in the 1960s or early 1970s. More recently, the term "chairman" was seen as sexist and replaced by "chairperson" and then simply "chair.") For the time being, at least, Wayne will continue to do what he does best.

Several aspects of Wayne's career stand out. First, his university life is bounded by the Department of Psychology. He has no sustained contact with professors in other fields and little with many in his own department. He interacts extensively with psychologists at other universities who do research on matters that interest him. Second, Wayne's research is narrow. He established a research niche as a young graduate student and has never strayed from his original interests. His experiments are far removed from larger questions of human existence. Third, effective undergraduate teaching is not a concern for Wayne. He tries hard in the classroom but emits no passion. He is not contemptuous of undergraduate students – they are simply not his priority. Even as a graduate student, Wayne was taught that research is a professor's first priority. He took the lesson to heart.

COMMENTS ON THE BIOGRAPHY

The first noteworthy feature of our fictional biography is that it is a biography of a professor, not a dean, or a president, or a provincial minister of education. Most strikingly, it is not a biography of a student, even though most of us would suppose that students are the most essential component of the university. We examined a professor for two main reasons. The first and less important reason is that many people – including people with university degrees – don't know how a person becomes a professor, what the various ranks of professor (assistant, associate, full) signify, what tenure is all about, what professors do with their time when they're not in the classroom, or what motivates professors. Telling a brief story about an imaginary, but quite typical, professor can clarify some of these matters.

There is a second, more important reason for discussing a professor. A central claim of this book is that Canadian universities are dominated in most important matters by the preferences of their tenured professors. Obviously, this does not mean that boards of governors immediately (or ever) accede to professors' salary demands. Nor does it deny the tremendous complexity of a modern Canadian university. But it does mean that professors' views are decisive on most major questions.[1] For example, professors decide who will be professors. They decide who will receive tenure, who will be promoted, and who will receive merit pay, as well as at what rate. Professors, not students or administrators or governments, decide what determines satisfactory (or unsatisfactory) performance in both general and specific ways. Professors have considerable influence over the choice of their superiors, notably department heads, deans of faculties, and even vice-presidents. With few restrictions they decide what courses they want to teach and the specific content of each course. Professors determine standards for the PhD students, the priority between teaching and research, and the role of nontenured professors. In other words, professors determine the curriculum, the composition of the professoriate itself, and the standards by which professors and students are evaluated. This short, illustrative list reveals a potent roster of important questions where professorial opinions hold sway.

Universities have a formal hierarchy of authority according to which a board of governors (which in Canada is appointed, in whole or in part, by the provincial government) stands above the president; the president stands above the vice-presidents (and their various associates and assistants); the vice-president (Academic), who is the senior vice-president; stands above the deans (and their bureaucrats); the deans stand above the department heads; and department heads stand above the professors in departments.

This formal view of universities holds some truths. For example, a determined dean may be able to mould certain features of one or two departments to his liking. But he cannot bring about changes that run contrary to the deepest convictions of an overwhelming majority of the professors in his faculty.[2] For example, a dean of arts can merge the Departments of Classics and Religious Studies, but he can't increase the teaching responsibilities of sociologists or insist that the English department have more courses on poetry than on science fiction, or require economists to assign essays.

Students are not a major force in Canadian universities, although they have some influence. They can and do vote with their feet. Departments of Classics, which study ancient civilizations, notably those of Greece and Rome, were once big items; now they are tiny or merged with larger units. In contrast, Faculties of Business, which used to have weak students, now have high entrance standards and attract far more students than they can admit. Still, students have to put up with huge, impersonal lectures, multiple-choice and fill-in-the-blanks examinations, and advanced undergraduate courses that have much more to do with the professors' research interests than the students' need or wants. Research reigns. Professors want it that way.

A second key in Wayne's story is that a successful academic career depends on one's recognized ability as a researcher. At every stage, Wayne's progress depended on the judgment of others that his scientific promise or achievement was high. He was recruited into the honours psychology program at York. While he was doing his MA, a distinguished professor at Toronto took an interest in his work and recommended him to several prestigious American universities. At Yale, the famous J.J. Stevens became his mentor. Then he came under the wing of Kathleen Johnson at the University of Alberta, where his quality was judged by his performance in her lab. He went to the top of the list for the coveted job at McMaster largely because his scientific achievements and promise were given top grades by Stevens and Johnson. At all points in his career at McMaster, Wayne's progress was dictated by his reputation as a scholar as assessed above all by the number of papers he published, the number and value of research grants he received, and by his reputation as a productive researcher. Research success enabled him to attract graduate students and get grants for further research, which enabled him to publish more papers, which drew more grants and graduate students, and so on. The central importance of research is revealed most starkly in the process of promotion to full professor, where a decisive factor is the evaluations of external referees who know the candidate only through his research. For these outsiders, teaching does not have a low weight; it has no weight.

Consider the role of research in Wayne's life. He teaches, at most, two courses each term (September to December, January to April), that is, six hours per week in the classroom for a little more than six months a year. He is a conscientious but experienced teacher, so he spends another six hours a week preparing for classes. (Preparation time was much greater in his early years of teaching.) He grades no essays (there are none in his courses), and he marks no examinations (they are all machine scored). The supervision and evaluation of lab assignments are done by his TAs. Supervising these TAs takes up two hours a week. He takes his role as graduate advisor for the Department of Psychology very seriously; in particular, he maintains regular office hours, and he goes out of his way to assist graduate students who are having problems. He spends eight hours a week on the duties connected with this position. Other administrative responsibilities take up no more than an hour a week. Consultations with postdoctoral students and supervision of graduate students not connected with his lab work takes up another three hours a week. So, for slightly more than six months a year, Wayne spends about twenty-six hours a week on academic matters other than research.

The caricature of the professor as a kindly, befuddled person with too much time on his hands bears about the same relationship to current reality as that of the newspaper reporter who, press badge in his fedora, exposes the wrongdoing of bad guys. Most professors work hard, and, in this regard, Wayne is typical. To the twenty-six hours a week he works on matters other than research, add *at least* another twenty-six for the various components of research. These include directing personnel in the laboratory, writing scientific papers in collaboration with associates, reading articles in scientific periodicals related to his own work, applying for research grants, keeping track of expenditures from existing research grants, attending conferences, and evaluating manuscripts sent to him for peer review. Wayne puts in these twenty-six hours a week of research during the six-plus months of the academic year. He takes the full month of vacation that is allotted to him by contract. This leaves over five months in which he has no teaching duties (a reduction of six hours in the classroom and six of preparation for class), and in which his other nonresearch duties are reduced by at least two-thirds. So for over five months of the year, forty-seven of Wayne's fifty-two hours a week of work are devoted exclusively to research. Over the year, then, something like 55 percent of Wayne's working time is spent on research, with the remainder divided among all his other duties. Wayne is a researcher first . . . and second . . . and third.

Wayne spends considerable time in the September to April period doing research. Sometimes this leads him to leave campus to attend conferences and to meet with like-minded researchers at other universities. During such absences, which are not regulated by universities, Wayne either cancels classes or labs or delegates his teaching responsibilities to a graduate student. Wayne is reasonably conscientious about his teaching and does not abuse his privileges. But it is not unheard of for professors to leave campus for several weeks during term. It is commonplace to cancel classes at least twice per term so that research-related travel can be undertaken.

Many people think that professors have "all summer off." By this they generally mean either that professors golf and vacation all summer or that they leisurely prepare for the return of students in September. Such views, which are held even by those with high awareness of other dimensions of university life, reveal the lingering stereotype of universities as quiet places of instruction. Wayne thrives in the summer and works fiercely. He is free to pursue his research unfettered by students, by exams, and by the obligations of the hectic September to April period.

The final point we want to make here about Wayne's story concerns teaching. When senior undergraduates or beginning graduate students start to think about becoming university professors they often say that they are "thinking about going into teaching." As Wayne's story reveals, they are doing little of the sort, at least in fields like his. Wayne was invited to join the honours program at York, admitted to the MA program at Toronto and the PhD program at Yale, hired at McMaster, and then moved swiftly through the ranks to full professor because of his promise and achievement as a scientific psychologist. The only point at which teaching played an important role was in the tenure decision, and then the requirement was adequacy, not high quality. It is also noteworthy that Wayne was never given any instruction in teaching nor was his teaching ability and promise evaluated before he entered the classroom as a professor. The assumption (which is dubious in the extreme) is that a graduate student acquires teaching know-how in the course of developing an ever-narrower specialization as a scholar. However, this is not to say that teaching by graduate students plays no role in the working of the contemporary Canadian university. On the contrary, a majority of graduate students spends at least one year, and often as many as three, in the role of teaching assistant. TAs are essential for lab supervision, for marking lab assignments, and generally for advising students in large courses. Without their work, professors would have to spend almost all their time on matters related to teaching, and the overriding concentration on research would be eroded. Then the university would be a very different place from what it is now.

CONCLUSION

Contemporary Canadian universities are diverse and complex institutions. Therefore, we cannot take the fictional biography of one professor of psychology as perfectly representative of all professors. Professors differ not only in their personalities but also, to some extent, in the preoccupations that stem from their various disciplines. Nevertheless, we maintain that Wayne's career is broadly typical of all professors, be they biochemists, lawyers, or historians.

We must examine a number of features of Canadian universities other than the professors. Nevertheless, we think the professors are central. For the good things about Canadian universities they deserve most of the credit. For the bad things they deserve most of the blame. Therefore, we have to look more carefully at some of the themes that emerged in our discussion of Wayne. What is research? Is it all valuable? Does time spent on research mean time taken away from teaching? What is good university teaching? Do universities do enough to encourage good teaching? It looks as though both teaching and, especially, research may be subject to serious abuses. (Consider, for example, the possibility that some professors might neglect their other duties because research is the road to pay raises and promotions. For another example, think of the opportunity professors have to take credit for ideas that are not their own.) We must give some attention to moral issues that arise in universities. Above all, we must consider whether universities are places where professors have the opportunity and the encouragement to think broadly and deeply, so that they can help students do the same.

CHAPTER 4

UNIVERSITY TEACHING

Imagine that the elementary schools in your neighbourhood have decided to leave the teaching of kids in grades one and two to university students on temporary contracts. These student teachers have little or no experience teaching. They are unable to give full attention to their pupils because they must spend part of their time working on their university courses. In addition, they have morale problems because they are paid less than half the salary of a beginning full-time teacher, and their classes contain twice as many students – and often ten times as many – as those in higher grades. Full-time teachers, meanwhile, confine their teaching to smaller classes at the higher grades, especially the highest ones. These experienced teachers believe their talents should be devoted to pupils who have mastered the basics. Anyway, teaching advanced students is easier and more fun than struggling with beginners.

Parents would be outraged if elementary schools were organized on such principles. Educators who abandoned beginning students to inexperienced, temporary teachers would be denounced as stupid or negligent. Parents would demand prompt action from school boards, from school principals and, if necessary, from provincial governments to ensure beginning pupils received attentive teaching from experienced, highly motivated, well-paid teachers in classes small enough that children could get individual attention.

The situation imagined above may seem so ridiculous as to be pointless. But it is not pointless. It pretty much describes the present-day character of teaching in Canadian universities. Far too frequently, beginning students are taught by temporary, inexperienced, often part-time teachers, commonly designated "sessional lecturers." Such lecturers are paid low wages, have no job security, and spend a great deal of time trying to prepare academic papers for publication so that some day they might get a permanent university position.

In a way, the situation in universities is worse than the one in the public schools we imagined above. If university students taught in the public schools, at least they would be students in a Faculty of Education, where most of their studies deal with the theory and practice of teaching. In contrast, sessional lecturers (like university professors) typically receive no instruction or practice in teaching whatsoever. Universities simply assume that if you are a competent chemistry or history graduate student you are fit to teach introductory university courses in chemistry or history. While the introductory courses are taught largely by sessional lecturers, advanced, specialized courses with smaller enrolments are taught by tenured professors. These specialized courses relate to professors' research interests, which they pursue devoutly. Professors neither seek nor profess broad understanding of the world or even the part of it covered by their own discipline. Professors seek and profess expertise not wisdom. This yields a strange and perverse scenario: experienced professors, who have had time to reflect on the nature, problems, and prospects of their subject and its relationships to other subjects, generally teach specialized courses to small classes, while inexperienced sessional lecturers deal with basic questions in large classes.

Teaching, especially the teaching of undergraduate students in their first two years of university, is extremely important. Yet it is not accorded the importance it deserves in contemporary Canadian universities. This chapter elaborates these opinions and rejects the view that the status quo in Canadian universities is just fine. The chapter has three main concerns. First, we argue that teaching should be recognized as preeminently important in Canadian universities. Second, we show that much of it ranges from indifferent to abysmal. Third, we address a difficult question: if teaching is as bad as we say it is, why is it so little criticized?

THE PREEMINENCE OF TEACHING

It is tempting to maintain that the preeminence of teaching among the tasks performed by universities is axiomatic: a point that is self-evident rather than one that needs to be defended. This is the position taken in the best discussion of Canadian universities whose authors state that "the first priority for the university is its teaching. This should be axiomatic, not needing to be argued for."[1] In a brutally realistic sense, this view is certainly true. Canada wouldn't have any universities – citizens wouldn't support them – if universities didn't teach.

However, many observers of modern universities deny that teaching should be the first priority of universities. Such observers seldom argue that universities should simply be research institutes. They acknowledge that teaching is an important function of universities. They simply deny that it is the preeminent function. Those who hold this view generally maintain that published research is as important as, or more often, far more important than, teaching. They argue that professors who do not publish research frequently in scholarly periodicals should not be professors. In the unfortunate event that such an unproductive person is hired, he or she should be considered deadwood and denied raises in salary and promotions. This outlook gave rise to the academic saying: "Publish or perish." We argue forcefully against this view.

Why Teaching Is Preeminent
Fortunately, reasons for the priority of teaching over research are readily available. The first reason is that research worthy of publication presupposes a lengthy program of learning, which requires competent teachers. Even those who stress publication acknowledge that newly minted high school graduates are not prepared to produce high-quality academic research. Professors expect that students must have at least one degree before they publish scholarly work. The main point of the PhD degree is to ease promising apprentices into frontier research by ensuring that their first sustained research effort is guided by an experienced research professor. Thus, even for budding researchers, teaching is both logically and temporally prior to publication.

The common response to the foregoing argument is that you can't teach what you don't know. The implication of this response is that research is in a way preeminent after all. In our view, this response is correct, but it does not support the case of the "publish or perish" advocates. Teaching students who have not achieved mastery of their subject does not require professors who are actively engaged in frontier research, which aims to discover new facts. Especially in the early years of study, university students need the breadth and depth offered by teachers who engage in the kind of research we call reflective inquiry. We discuss reflective inquiry at greater length in the next chapter. For now it is sufficient to point out that reflective inquiry aims at achieving largeness of vision. The reflective inquirer seeks to grasp the history, nature, and limits of his own subject, its strength and weaknesses, and its relationship to other subjects, including those both · near and far from his own. For example, the reflective physicist is familiar with the main stages in the evolution of his subject, the nature and inter-relationships of the various specialties within the discipline, the relationship of physics to subjects such as chemistry, mathematics, and engineering. He has also thought about the associations (or lack thereof) between physics, theology, biology, and politics. Good teaching certainly presupposes this kind of research. But this kind of research is seldom advocated by those who stress publication. Reflective inquiry contributes more to wisdom and good teaching than to academic publications. It is thus more closely allied to good teaching than to the research advocated by "publish or perish" enthusiasts and therefore supports the case for the preeminence of teaching.

The foregoing argument rests on a characterization of undergraduate students that we expand upon in order to demonstrate further the pre-eminence of teaching in the university. In our view, most undergraduate students have neither the aptitude nor the inclination to engage in research of any kind. This point is almost too obvious to mention in regard to the vocational faculties. Practically everyone who enters medicine does so in order to become a practising doctor, law in order to become a working lawyer, and engineering in order to design bridges, pipelines, or commu-nications satellites. What is true of medicine, law, and engineering is also true for education, nursing, journalism, occupational therapy, forestry, physical education, and, of course, business. Students who enter these fac-ulties consciously set themselves on a specific career path. Their aims are practical. What they seek from university is the facts, lore, know-how, and polish to pursue successful careers. For this purpose they have no need to do research themselves (beyond the kind of research we all do when we find out which peonies are hardy in our climate zone or which washing machines have a good record of reliability). Their professors require little more. Of course, they must keep up with recent developments in their fields. However, this does not require groundbreaking research aimed at publication; it needs only the most elementary form of reflective inquiry.

What about students in the large Faculties of Arts and Science? Except for those who occupy places in these parts of the university only until they qualify to enter a professional faculty, arts and science students are seldom careerists like those in the professional faculties. Although they are aware that the lifetime earnings of university graduates are significantly higher than those of people without degrees, students in anthropology, botany, drama, mathematics, and Romance languages are often more interested in expanding their intellects and sensibilities than in getting on with a job. Do they or their teachers need to engage in groundbreaking research? Certainly not for the sake of the students' first couple of years of university.

Before we even begin to discuss the strictly academic part of their lives, we should consider briefly the huge burden of social adaptation that falls upon students as they enter Canadian universities. On entering university, many students enter a small city that is more populous, and certainly more anonymous, than their hometowns. Even students from big cities, where they are among the majority who enter university directly from high school, confront the shock of anonymity. Students spend at least a year adjusting to the impersonality and other peculiarities of university routine. Moreover, in the past couple of decades, more students have devoted more time to part-time jobs, often as a matter of financial necessity and often as a matter of enjoying amenities like an apartment away from home, fashionable clothes, and a good car. Thus, more beginning university students now make adjustments that were not common two decades ago.

We turn now to the academic dimension of the beginning students' lives. The first couple of years of their academic careers are devoted to acquiring basic facts (What is the structure of an atom? How are candidates for public office recruited in India?), developing skills (calculus, formal logic, statistics, types of experimentation, adept use of a major library, computer literacy, clear expository writing), and getting a feel for the rudiments of properly sceptical but certainly not cynical thinking. Neither students nor their teachers have to do frontier research in order to acquire these abilities, although an effective teacher will help students cultivate a capacity for reflective inquiry.

What about the final two years of arts and science programs? Does frontier research begin to assume a central place then? It does not, except for a few unusual students in the sciences (and even fewer in the social sciences) who develop a deep interest in experimentation or field study.[2] More commonly, advanced undergraduate students who become deeply interested in their studies exhibit little interest in the minutiae of painstaking empirical or textual investigations. They are drawn to the large questions of reflective inquiry: Is the Big Bang theory correct? Is there life on other planets? Is meteorology irremediably inexact? Are there innate psychological differences between women and men? Are stock markets really efficient? Students fascinated by such questions are not good candidates for teachers preoccupied with publishing new findings. On the contrary, these students need teachers who "specialize" in breadth, taking moral and political commitment seriously, and developing the cultivation of imagination and critical thinking. In short, they need teachers whose vocation is reflective inquiry.

We hope we have made a convincing case for the preeminence of teaching. No matter how strong our case, however, it is not widely accepted by Canadian professors or university administrators. Much teaching in Canadian universities ranges from indifferent to abysmal. We defend this assertion at some length below. However, in order to make a strong case that much of the teaching in Canadian universities is weak, we must first explain what we mean by good teaching.

DIMENSIONS OF GOOD TEACHING

A plausible answer to the question, "What is good university teaching?" must concentrate on what good teachers do, rather than on their personal qualities. Of course certain personal qualities are indispensable: intelligence, curiosity, and imagination are certainly on the list. But there is no personality profile of a good teacher. Some good teachers are introverts and some are extroverts, some are mercurial and some are phlegmatic, some are distant and some are warm. These are only a few of the respects in which good teachers differ in personality. Fortunately, good teachers have a great deal in common in what they do (and what they don't do), regardless of their personality type.

The Minimum Condition

Good teachers always meet the minimum requirement of teaching, which is to be where students have a right to expect them to be. This point may seem so obvious that the very mention of it is a wisecrack. Unfortunately, in contemporary Canadian universities, it is no wisecrack. There are several places where students have a right to expect professors to be. The first, of course, is the designated classroom during the designated time period. The second is the designated times and places for meeting students outside the classroom. This includes, at minimum, ample and convenient office hours and, in addition, being available, with no other pressing duties, at least one half-day per week.[3] Of course, there are occasions when these duties need not − indeed should not − be fulfilled. Illness, death of a family member, and various emergencies are obvious examples. We will show later in this chapter how even this minimum requirement is often violated without an appropriate excuse.

Knowing the Subject

That a good university teacher must know his subject is likely to command universal assent. After all, who wants to be exposed to a teacher who doesn't know his subject? But what does it really mean to say that a teacher knows his subject? If Professor Canes teaches a course called Introductory Economics, is he required to "know economics"? Must he exhibit mastery of the economic history of the world, close familiarity with the history of economic theory, and detailed understanding of disagreements among econometricians, to mention only a few "parts" of economics? The answer is surely, No, this is not what we mean by "knowing your subject" in the context of an introductory course − or any other, for that matter. No one can master all the fields of economics; perhaps no one can master even one field.

If a professor can "know his subject" without mastering it, is it good enough if he stays a couple of jumps ahead of his students, so that if they are working on Chapter 7 of the textbook he is on Chapter 9? Again, surely not: this is a shift from the outrageously demanding to the pathetically inadequate. However, if mastery, on the one hand, and being a short step ahead of the students, on the other hand, are unacceptable extremes, what is the golden mean for the teacher of introductory economics? This question, as we suggested earlier, is best answered by indicating what good teachers do (or are prepared to do if asked). The teacher of introductory economics lays out the fundamental principles (axioms and unchallenged presuppositions) of economics. He explains how these principles manifest themselves in various spheres of economic life, such as banking, international trade, and the determination of income and savings. Since corporations and labour unions are social and political as well as economic institutions, he explains the relationships between economics, sociology, and political science. He has apt examples at his fingertips and knows when and how to use them. He has often thought about the tough questions students often ask. Thus, he is not speechless if a student asks: "Did the collapse of the Soviet system prove that socialism is unworkable?" or "Does the trucking industry pay its fair share of the cost of maintaining roads?" The economist's ability to answer these questions shows that part of "knowing his field" is knowing not only where economists agree and why, but also knowing where and why they disagree. The foregoing sketch of knowing the field for purposes of an introductory economics course is applicable to other economics courses and to courses in other fields. In astronomy, nursing, or English, the university professor knows her subject if she can lay out its basic principles and explain how these principles manifest themselves in various branches of the subject, understands broadly the relationship between her subject and others, and is well equipped with good examples and grasps both the agreements and disagreements among practitioners of her subject so that she can answer tough questions from students. The vast majority of Canadian professors would deserve good grades for knowledge of subject if knowledge of subject were a matter of expertise in a narrow subfield of their subject (for example, as Hardy's poetry is a narrow subfield of English). However, few professors know their subject well as we described it above. Acquiring such knowledge is extremely time-consuming – and never-ending.

Teaching Ideas Rather Than Information

Although it is necessary for a good teacher to know his subject, it is certainly not sufficient. In this regard, consider the most common student complaint: "Professor So-and-so is a brilliant man, but he just can't get his ideas across." Sometimes saying that the professor is brilliant is just a polite way of taking the sting out of the judgment that he is a poor teacher. More often, students assume that because So-and-so has lots of degrees, if they can't understand him it must be because he is unimaginably profound, rather than arrogant, preoccupied with research, unaware that he is failing to communicate, or simply uninterested in teaching. Still, it is true that some professors know their subject but don't teach it well. A number of things can go wrong and lead to this result. The most common problem is teaching facts rather than ideas.

Few activities are more damaging to higher education than teaching that takes the form of reciting facts or findings. This is not to say that facts and findings are unimportant. It is to say that their importance derives exclusively from their place in a structure of ideas – for example, as axioms, or supporting evidence, or contradictions of a theory, or consistent with an interesting hypothesis. The good teacher doesn't tell students that Mexico City is the world's largest city unless this is part of an important theory, hypothesis, conjecture, or declamation about urbanization, or Latin America, or social class in poor countries, or some other consequential matter. Similarly for findings about the comparative frequency of blinking by women and men, the occurrence of earthquakes in Asia, and the verdicts in court cases arising under section 15 of the Canadian Charter of Rights and Freedoms.

In short, good teachers always examine arguments; they do not dispense information. As we use the term, arguments are not squabbles, though they may give rise to squabbles and may be used by squabblers. Arguments are simply trains of reasoning in which a conclusion is derived from certain premises. The classic example is the derivation of the conclusion "Socrates is mortal" from the premises "All men are mortal" and "Socrates is a man." Of course, the chains of reasoning examined in university courses – for example, those used to support the wave theory of light or the fairness conception of justice – are more complex, and more interesting, than the classic about Socrates. Facts are certainly not irrelevant. Even in the classic case the argument fails if some men are immortal or Socrates is a hamster. The point is that facts alone, or facts that support only trivial conclusions, are worth no one's time. In regard to the classic case, for example, it is irrelevant to anything (as far as we know) that Socrates got on badly with his wife or that his pulse rate was abnormal. Similarly, without the context of an argument, it is unimportant where asthma rates are high and low, that Bertrand Russell wrote over 100 books, or that an overwhelming majority of professional basketball players are black. Good teachers never smother arguments with information.

Enthusiasm

We have interviewed professors and students about what makes a good university teacher and enthusiasm is invariably either at the top or close to the top of the list. Enthusiasm sometimes manifests itself in the kind of ebullience you see the first time a child manages to ride a bike. However, this is not common. More often a teacher's passion is quite restrained. The late C.B. Macpherson of the University of Toronto, Canada's greatest political theorist, was so restrained that some students missed the passion altogether. Be it a large lecture or a small seminar, Macpherson read in a flat voice from a meticulously prepared script, eyes fixed on his notes, no language coming from an apparently uncomfortable body. However, there was an intensity in his voice that told anyone who listened that he believed deeply that understanding the ideas of seventeenth-century philosophers was important, and that he could aid that understanding. Moreover, when he was asked a challenging question, his concentration deepened still further, and he answered the question clearly, at length, and with obvious relish. Teachers can manifest enthusiasm in many ways, but without enthusiasm even a person who knows his subject very well cannot be a good teacher. As students often ask, "If the professor doesn't care about the subject, why should I?"

Treating Students with Respect

A professor can be faultless in her knowledge of her subject yet still fail to be a good teacher if she does not show respect for her students. This statement is largely uncontroversial in Canadian universities. Given broad support for feminism and multiculturalism, most professors are extremely careful to avoid possible charges of sexism, racism, or ethnocentrism. Although this may lead some timid professors to be too cautious in the short run, its desirability is undeniable. The problem is not with professors exhibiting respect for students through increased attentiveness to sexual and ethnic diversity but with seeing this as the only dimension of respect. That it certainly is not. In particular, respect for students generally prohibits public humiliation of students. (Warranted private criticism may cause embarrassment, guilt, or shame. So be it.) Hardly anything is more antithetical to education than putting down a student in public, since there is no surer way of ensuring that both the student in question and his classmates will disengage from the course even if they don't formally withdraw. And putting down does not just consist in aggressively boorish conduct such as labelling a student's question "stupid." It can also involve brushing off a student's request for further clarification or responding to it as though it were a huge burden to deal with a matter so mundane.

Respect for students requires criticism as well as encouragement. In any sphere of life, not just teaching, you undermine rather than enhance a person's dignity if you say that he is doing well if he isn't. Pop psychology self-esteem hucksters insist that self-esteem is all-important and that it is sustained and strengthened only by praise. Both these claims are false, especially the second. Self-esteem based on unwarranted praise is phony self-esteem that we are all better without. Moreover, it is impossible to see how lying to a person about his qualities or achievements (or lack thereof) is showing respect for him. Specifically in regard to teaching, good teachers stimulate students to improve, and this requires honest assessment: both encouragement and criticism.

Finally, the most important dimension of treating students with respect is taking them as they are, not as they would be if their high school curriculum had been better, or their high school teachers cared more about science than punctuality, or the students weren't so concerned about grades, or they had learned more in their English course about writing and less about popular culture, or they took courses only from the smart professors in your department rather than from the mediocre, and so on. Good teachers complain as much as bad ones, maybe more. However, they do not confuse their fantasies about ideal students with the ones they actually teach. For example, they do not teach Shakespeare as though students were already deeply familiar with several of his plays or symbolic logic as though students were already accomplished mathematicians.

Of course, it is possible to aim too low as well as too high, and underestimating students' achievements and possibilities is as disrespectful as overestimating them. Professors should stimulate students to the best work of which they are capable. Thus, taking students as they are does not mean resting satisfied with students as they are. It means motivating them to fulfil their potentialities, something the professor-as-information-dispenser ignores. This point leads to a particularly revealing test of good teaching. In every undergraduate university class, some students, probably 20 percent, are both exceptionally intelligent and highly motivated. Five percent lack either intelligence, or motivation, or both to such a degree that they are unteachable. Ten percent defy any teacher to induce them to think deeply about anything. The good teacher teaches all but the utterly hopeless 5 percent. Naturally she concentrates on the 65 percent who are able and motivated and who most want and need attentive teaching. The 10 percent of know-nothings should be the least of her worries. Every good teacher rightly wants to reach them and transform them, and this is not futile because there are occasional successes. But the good teacher does not allow them to take up much time that could be spent helping the students who not only need help but also want it. The top 20 percent need close attention least because they can learn so much on their own. But good teachers do not ignore them since these students too benefit from guidance and stimulation. The particularly revealing test of good teaching posed by this diversity of students is the success or failure of the teacher in giving due attention to all but the hopeless of them.

We have identified five characteristics of good university teachers based on what they do rather than on their personality traits. First, good teachers are present when and where students have a right to expect them to be. Second, good teachers know their subject. Third, they teach ideas rather than information, so that they examine arguments rather than state facts. Fourth, they are enthusiastic about their subject and eager that students share their enthusiasm. Finally, good teachers always treat students with respect.

University teaching, far from being a tedious obligation that distracts professors from exciting research, is a rewarding, complex, and labour-intensive activity. Good university teachers think constantly about their subject, the role of teaching, and the needs of their students. Analysis of any of the characteristics of good teaching reveals the underlying complexity. For example, we argue that good professors are always respectful of their students. However, students are a heterogeneous group with different interests, motivations, and skills. Their needs are seldom self-evident. Insecure students sometimes mask their anxieties with bravado. Extraordinarily committed students sometimes appear apathetic and detached. Only experience, reflection, and considerable personal effort allow professors to properly understand their students. Such examples could be multiplied.

BAD TEACHING

Unfortunately, some professors have personalities that prevent them from being adequate, let alone good, teachers. Common frailties are painful shyness, inability to accept criticism or even disagreement, and lack of a sense of humour. Only a small minority of professors suffers from these misfortunes, however. It follows that, if they *did* the right things, the overwhelming majority of university teachers would be pretty good at worst and many would be very good or excellent.[4] But much of the teaching in Canadian universities ranges from indifferent to abysmal. This section explains why this is so.

Unavailability

Those who have never been to university, or attended some years ago, may assume that our first criterion of good teaching – that the teacher be present where and when students have a right to expect him to be – is met almost without exception. It is met almost without exception by sessional lecturers. Many professors, however, do not come close to meeting it. They often miss classes without a pressing reason. Their office hours are at best barely adequate. And when they are not obliged to be available, their closed office doors are ample evidence of the welcome intruders will receive.

Are these professors lazy? Far from it. Of all the vices to which professors are subject, indolence is one of the rarest. Professors do not fulfil their obligations to students because they are too busy, not because they are too lazy. We use the term "busy" advisedly to emphasize that most professors hustle and bustle collecting and collating information. Contemplation, reflection, and speculation are not high priorities for modern professors. Professors prosper to the extent that they are "productive professionals." A recent, increasingly common, practice of productive professionals is to hold conferences on weekdays during the academic year, rather than confining them to weekends or the summer. Professors who attend these conferences invariably miss one or more of their classes. More important than missing classes is stinting on office hours and being unavailable outside office hours for consultations with students and colleagues. We attribute this to the usual culprit: immense university pressure to do research, get grants, and above all, publish articles in learned journals. The pressure to publish is greatest on younger, nontenured professors and so they are generally the ones who spend the least time with their office doors open to whomever may wish to consult them. The prospect, therefore, is that the problem will worsen rather than improve as professors mature believing that students have little call on their time.

Ignorance of the Subject
Contemporary Canadian university professors are certainly not ignorant. They know a great deal. The problem is that, as the old saw goes, they know more and more about less and less. The majority of modern professors are experts not generalists. For example, a professor of medicine in the Department of Infectious Diseases would not dream of teaching a course about all such diseases or even a wide range of them. She would teach about whatever is her field of professional practice and research: hepatitis B, or malaria, or influenza. Indeed, it is common practice for courses in infectious diseases to be taught by a group of professors, each dealing with his or her specialty. Such extreme specialization is less common outside the sciences, but even in the humanities many professors are uncomfortable outside their specialties: Central American novelists, eighteenth-century English social history, or postcolonial feminism.

Extreme specialists, who yearly increase their numbers, status, and influence in Canadian universities, usually do not know their subjects in the way we described earlier as important for teaching undergraduates. We said that university professors know their subjects if they can lay out the basic principles, explain how these principles manifest themselves in various branches of the subject, understand broadly the relationship between the subject and others, are well equipped with clear examples, and grasp both the agreements and disagreements among practitioners of their subject so that they can answer tough questions from students. Few if any professors (certainly including the authors of this book) know their subject as well as they should. However, it is increasingly rare now for professors even to aspire to know their subjects in this way. Many younger professors try to confine their teaching to advanced, specialized courses so that breadth is not required, or so they believe. Professors who cannot (or will not) teach first- and second-year students are not good teachers.

Teaching As a Necessary Evil

Good teachers exhibit enthusiasm for their subjects and for the opportunity to encourage others to share their passion. But we have already noted that university professors and administrators invariably speak of teaching "loads" and research "opportunities." These words are worth a thousand pictures in revealing prevailing attitudes toward teaching. Teaching, in this view, is an onerous task performed only because it is necessary to do the enjoyable stuff: research. It would seem to follow that enthusiasm is focused entirely on research not on teaching. This is not entirely true, however. Most professors who are absorbed by frontier research like to teach courses directly related to their research to small, advanced classes of students who share the professor's interests. These courses are commonly taught with considerable enthusiasm. The losers are the vast majority of students who must cope with the indifference or boredom of these specialist professors when they "teach" larger, less specialized courses.

The puzzling question is not why so many basic courses are taught nonchalantly or worse but why some are taught with dedication and verve. The answer must be that a minority of professors differs from their colleagues in their beliefs and attitudes about teaching. They must either believe in the preeminence of teaching or, at least, that teaching is so important that some research time should be given up for the sake of it. They must also feel intensely the elation that comes from teaching well and that this makes up for the distress that follows a poor performance.[5] Attentive teaching is no longer a matter of duty; it is a matter of conscience.

Bloated Classes

In Canadian universities, many classes for first- and second-year students contain more than 100 students, and it is not uncommon for such classes to contain 500 or more. Class size sometimes exceeds 50 even in the third and fourth years of some programs. Good teaching, we maintain, is impossible in classes of this size. For one thing, the teacher cannot concentrate on ideas and arguments in this setting. Speaking through a microphone and relying heavily on visual aids – some teachers of huge classes include rock music and light shows in their arsenals – these lecturers have no choice but to state lore to be imbibed rather than to discuss theories, hypotheses, and conjectures to be considered critically. Subtlety stands about as much chance in this sort of class as it does in daytime television. The proof of this is that evaluation of students in classes of this sort invariably takes the form of "objective" (multiple-choice and true or false) tests and examinations. Evaluations of this type are incapable of assessing students' abilities to engage in complex trains of reasoning, recognize subtleties, or exercise moral or aesthetic judgment.

In gigantic classes, teachers cannot convey their enthusiasm for the subject or their love of learning and critical thinking. In a class of several hundred in an auditorium, professors cannot make eye contact with anyone farther back than the fifth row. They must therefore use showbiz as a surrogate for passion.

Huge classes are inimical to critical thinking and the fostering of love of learning. They are also incompatible with treating students with respect. Admittedly, there is no way of humiliating students in a huge class. However, this benefit is heavily outweighed by the impossibility of stimulating and encouraging them. Moreover, it is impossible to provide students in huge classes with constructive criticism. Finally, and most important, in huge classes, the professor cannot tailor his teaching to the needs of the diverse body of students in his charge. In particular, since he cannot answer questions at all, he certainly can't answer the diverse questions that occur to students of vastly different levels of intelligence and experience. Huge classes are not teaching environments at all. They are daycare centres for adults.

Large classes have terrible flaws. But Canadian universities continue to use them and even to argue that large classes are not necessarily worse than small ones. A well-known Canadian statement of this view is the short article, "Quality Education: Does Class Size Matter?" by sociologist Sid Gilbert.[6] Gilbert reviews some studies about class sizes and teaching and concludes that course content, organization, and instructor ability are more important than size. He maintains that large classes have some "positive features" compared with small ones. Moreover, the "negative features" of large classes can be minimized by proper technique. However, his reasoning is utterly unconvincing. The "positive" features of large classes are dubious and their "negative" features are to be remedied by making them like (or seem like) small classes.

The positive aspects of large classes, Gilbert tells us, are: "the presence of other students, low pressure, sense of independence, and anonymity of attendance." These "aspects" are bizarre. Large classes are characterized by the presence of other students. Yup. Lots of them. What about small classes? Are they characterized by the *absence* of other students? Seemingly not, for then they would be nonexistent classes not small classes. What is "low pressure"? It can't be lack of encouragement to work hard, think deeply, and learn much, since that would certainly not be a "positive aspect"; it would be a shameful failure. "Sense of independence"? We simply don't know what this means. It must not be the same as actually being independent. Is it a feeling (possibly illusory) that one is independent? Perhaps so. But then what is "positive" about it? The final alleged "positive aspect" is "anonymity of attendance." We guess this means that the professor will never know if students attend class or not. If this were true, it is not obvious that it is a good thing. It might be, but Gilbert doesn't tell us how or why. However, we need not let that bother us, since the claim is certainly false. There is no great difficulty in taking attendance in large classes: teaching assistants can be assigned the task and sometimes are. Furthermore, many teachers of smaller classes pay no attention to attendance.

The techniques recommended for remedying "negative aspects" of large classes amount to making those classes more like small ones or, worse, duping students into believing that big classes have the intimacy of small ones. One technique recommended for reducing impersonality in large classes is occasionally dividing large classes into small study or working units. This is fine as far as it goes, but it is clearly an admission that large classes are better the more they are like small classes, which is exactly our point. Gilbert mentions two other methods of ensuring "meaningful contact with students in a large class." First, he states that "remaining in the lecture hall for a few minutes after class can do a lot to convince students that you are interested in them." Second, he reports approvingly that the feelings of insignificance and anonymity students may sense in a large classroom can be mitigated by following the example of an instructor who "reports using a cordless microphone that allows him to lecture while wandering around the classroom." The purpose of both of these techniques seems to be to hoodwink students into believing that the professor has a deep personal interest in every one of them. Leaving aside the morality of such deceit, we find it hard to believe that students would be taken in by it.

The core of the case for large classes comes down to the contention that the best large class is better than the worst small class. This point may be conceded readily. Bad classes are bad classes, no matter what their size. But that is not the question. The question is this: Given a conscientious, knowledgeable, thoughtful, enthusiastic professor who respects his students, will he be a better teacher in a class of 40 students or in a class of 400? The answer is too easy for words.

Gilbert states the crux of his case as follows: "In large classes students prefer experienced, qualified or very knowledgeable instructors." No doubt this is true. Does it follow, however, that in small classes students prefer – or are at least content with – inexperienced, unqualified, or ignorant instructors? Of course not. Proponents of huge courses know full well that their job is to make silk purses out of sows' ears.

If large classes are indefensible, why are they such prominent parts of modern Canadian universities? Why do universities continue to defend the indefensible? The answer to these questions is not far to seek. Large classes have two main advantages from the standpoint of professors. First, if there are large classes, there can be fewer of them. For example, if 1,500 students enroll in Chemistry 100, they can be accommodated in thirty classes of 50 students each. However, if the class size is raised to 250, only six classes are required. If large classes are the rule for first- and second-year chemistry students, chemistry professors can concentrate on teaching upper-level and graduate courses that are close to their research interests. More important, large lower-level courses allow them to keep their "teaching load" down to one or one-and-a-half courses per year. This allows them to spend the bulk of their time on research. In other words, universities choose large classes in order to facilitate research, a basic point that casts some doubt on, though it does not itself disprove, university complaints about underfunding.

Every Canadian university has a number of good teachers, some excellent teachers, and a handful of great teachers. Nevertheless, much teaching ranges from mediocre to abysmal. The institutional evidence of poor teaching is evident: There are too many large classes, especially at the crucial introductory level. Too many sessional lecturers are assigned to teach students in their first and second years, while tenured professors teach advanced courses with small classes. Many professors miss classes without good reason and otherwise do too little to make themselves available to students. The reasons for inattentive teaching are also evident. Most professors prefer research to teaching. They are rewarded in pay, promotion, and prestige for following their bent.

WHY STUDENTS DON'T COMPLAIN

The *Maclean's* 1992 university issue reported that one-third of 500 respondents to a nationwide survey of university students had unkind words to say about large classes. However, the same survey revealed that 83 percent of respondents regarded the quality of teaching they received as "good" or "excellent."[7] This apparent contradiction is perplexing. No less perplexing is the fact that a large majority of Canadian university students and recent graduates regularly evaluate their education as good to excellent. If what we have said in this chapter is correct, this flattering evaluation is undeserved. The question for us, then, is: Why are students apparently satisfied with university teaching and so short of complaints?

Three plausible answers present themselves. The first answer is that our analysis is wrong. Needless to say, we reject this diagnosis, not because we are incapable of making such a big mistake but because we have done our best to avoid doing so. We have reflected hard on the evidence and arguments. They force us to the conclusion that much teaching in universities ranges from mediocre to abysmal. In this regard, we remind readers that major American universities now admit that their undergraduate teaching is poor, although debate continues about why this is so. There is no reason to believe that Canadian universities differ in this key respect.

A second plausible response is that our analysis is correct and students know it but most of them won't say so publicly. Is this response credible? A couple of interrelated observations about current student attitudes could lend it support. First, for the most part, modern students are deeply conservative. Unlike some of their parents (actually a vociferous minority), who openly pressed professors to be "relevant" (that is, supportive of leftist causes), the overwhelming majority of current students is quiescent. They subscribe to the old formula: If you want to get along, go along. So they are disinclined to protest against the quality of teaching they receive. The second point is that we live in a period in which most people, including the vast majority of university students, think they are incapable of influencing elites that control society. They think it is a waste of time to protest – about universities or anything else – because complaints always fall on deaf ears.

These explanations are plausible but not convincing. Granted most Canadian university students today are quite conservative, perhaps even more so than in the 1950s. This would explain why there is no ranting and railing, let alone organized protests, against unsatisfactory teaching. However, it does not explain why students would lie about their opinions of their teachers in an anonymous poll. Similarly, there is little doubt that we are witnessing one of the periodic high points of disenchantment with the way elites run traditional institutions. For example, New Age folks are invading the turf of the churches, numerous forms of alternative medicine are making doctors uneasy, and bitter jokes about lawyers are widespread. Yet even the anti-elitist Canadian Alliance Party and its predecessor, the Reform Party, have not caught universities in their sights. Public opinion polls do not detect disenchantment with universities. Universities and their professors do not seem to be regarded with the same suspicion and contempt as other Canadian institutions and professions. In sum, the hypothesis that university students are unhappy with their professors but are unwilling to say so even anonymously is unconvincing.

Only one plausible explanation remains: a great deal of indifferent teaching goes unnoticed by many students. But how can this be? After all, one of the most important tools for assessing teaching is the student questionnaire at the end of each course. In making this point, we are neither dismissing questionnaires nor implying that students are stupid. We do maintain, however, that some characteristics of students and questionnaires cast doubt on the proposition that students believe that the majority of their professors are good to excellent.

Consider three points about students. First, university students are exposed to a great deal of university propaganda about teaching. For one thing, the mutual enrichment thesis (that teaching and research reinforce each other and that good teachers are good researchers) is preached in every corner of the university. Second, university spokespeople (not surprisingly) insist that teaching is taken very seriously at their university. Third, universities highlight the teaching awards they have begun to bestow in the past decade. Universities do not inform students that the mutual enrichment thesis is dubious at best, that they regard taking teaching seriously as consistent with taking research much more seriously, and that conferring awards on a few excellent teachers is quite compatible with undervaluing teaching in general. Students are bombarded by the idea that both universities as institutions and individual professors attach very high priority to teaching. These forces create a presumption that can be overcome only by powerful evidence to the contrary.

Second, good teaching as outlined earlier in this chapter is simply not a high priority for many students, although no student happily tolerates bad teaching. So-so teaching is widely accepted in the professional faculties, where the principal concern for most students is not intellectual distinction but the wherewithal to get a good job. For example, undergraduate engineers work very hard, but most of them look for vocational lore and skills rather than stimulation and the challenge of controversy in their courses. For another example, it is standard practice in law schools, facilitated by professors, for students to rely on "canned" notes to facilitate the assimilation of masses of information that must be quickly reproduced on both law school and bar admission examinations. For a final example, chemistry departments in big universities often put on special sections of courses for medical students, for the reason that many aspiring doctors are exceptionally intelligent, competitive, and hard working, yet often lacking in curiosity. Moreover, a vocational orientation is not confined to professional faculties. A sizable minority of students in the arts and sciences also has a primarily vocational orientation. Their interest is not in the academic part of the university experience but in the degree that they hope will lead to an interesting and remunerative career. In short, many students have little interest in the quality of teaching unless it is excruciatingly bad. This is another reason why we hear so few complaints about indifferent teaching in universities.

Our final and most important point is that students arrive at university with no concrete expectations about what higher education is, except that it is somehow tougher than high school, partly because professors are "smarter" and more demanding than high school teachers. When they discover that university isn't all that tough, that many professors aren't very smart, and that few are very demanding, they are in a weak position to criticize because they don't know what is reasonable to expect. Mediocre-to-bad university teaching is thus self-validating. Students, with no other basis on which to judge, infer that indifferent teaching is the norm and hence, at worst, good. Students who are fortunate enough to take a course from a very good or excellent teacher conclude that this teacher is exceptional, not that many other teachers could do better if they tried.

Consider now the questionnaires. Students are discouraged from complaining about unsatisfactory teaching by the structure and context of their most accessible medium for expressing their opinions about courses: the student questionnaire. Student questionnaires, mandatory in every course taught at many universities, are administered at the end of a course. They permit students to grade their teacher by posing questions about whether the teacher is good, bad, or indifferent in several respects. Typical questions concern the teacher's knowledge of the subject, whether the course was well organized, the availability of the teacher outside class, the willingness and ability of the teacher to answer questions, and the fairness of the grading. Invariably, questions ask respondents for an overall rating of the course and the teacher. By and large the questions are helpful and apt. (There are some exceptions. For example, the question whether the teacher knows her subject is very important but not one students are in a good position to answer.) Moreover, the standard criticism of these questionnaires – that they identify popular teachers (those who tell jokes and give high grades) rather than good ones – is unproved.

However, a serious problem arises with most student questionnaires. Typically, they take the form of making a statement and then asking the student to select from five possible responses to it. For example, the statement might be: "The instructor handles students' questions competently."

The available responses will be some version of: (1) agree strongly, (2) agree, (3) neither agree nor disagree, (4) disagree, (5) disagree strongly. This format results in a clustering of student responses such that only the superb teachers and the truly awful ones stand out. Consider that in the most common grading system teachers have available eleven grades: A+, A, A-, B+, B, B-, C+, C, C-, D, and F. This array allows considerable discrimination without a false appearance of exactitude. For example, B- and C+ are close, but there is a definite difference between them. With only five alternatives available, the average grades assigned to professors tend to converge just below the second highest category. The usual translation of the categories is (1) excellent, (2) very good, (3) good, (4) fair, (5) poor. As a result, average teachers are rated just short of "very good." Weak teachers are rated "good." Hopeless teachers are rated as "fair." No teachers are rated as "poor."

That said, we still have to ask, Why is the average so high? Why is it closer to 3.8 than 3.2? We don't need to psychoanalyze students to find the answer. If we want to know why they grade their teachers generously, we simply have to look at *their* grades. Grade inflation has been occurring in Canadian universities, following the pattern of elite American universities, for the last thirty years, and even more rapidly during the last twenty.[8] In the twenty-first century, students complain bitterly if they get a C on an assignment. They seldom challenge the assessment that the work is mediocre but only the view that mediocre work is worth less than a B-. Nowadays everyone who is admitted to a university passes every course if she exerts a modicum of effort. Moreover, even students with modest intellectual gifts can do very well if they work hard. Students seldom fail unless they quit without the formalities of official withdrawal. Since we treat them so generously, why would they treat us any worse? Just like our students, we don't fail, and worse than mediocre is good to very good. In short, another reason why university students don't complain is that there is an unwritten pact between them and their professors that neither teaching nor learning is bad unless it is horrible. There is no conspiracy here; there is unthinking acceptance of a mutually beneficial racket. In this regard, a perceptive American commentator has referred to the "faculty-student non aggression pact" that reigns even at the best universities in the United States.[9]

Much teaching in Canadian universities ranges from mediocre to abysmal but students do not complain loudly. Three main reasons explain students' silence. First, universities tirelessly insist that they take teaching very seriously, as exhibited by the now universal conferral of teaching awards. Second, a sizable number of students, mainly but not exclusively in the professional faculties, has little interest in good teaching. These students are upset only by bad teaching. Finally, the structure and context of the main vehicle of student assessment of teaching, the student course questionnaire, favours the identification of teachers who are either excellent or abominable but discourages the identification of those who are mediocre or worse.

CONCLUSION

Teaching should be the preeminent task of universities. The form of research that we call reflective inquiry is important for undergraduate teaching, but frontier research is not. Much of the teaching in Canadian universities ranges from mediocre to abysmal. This situation is utterly unacceptable. We now turn to university research, the activity whose pursuit has badly damaged the quality of teaching.

CHAPTER 5

RESEARCH AND REFLECTIVE INQUIRY

Competing Principles

This chapter explores research as the dominant force in Canadian universities. University research, a broad and complex phenomenon, is now said to be the university's lifeblood, its strength, and the basis of its prestige. Without research, the modern university is seen by its supporters to be nothing more than a glorified community college.

We challenge these views and argue that university research requires dispassionate analysis. The uncritical pursuit of research as a university priority has weakened universities' commitment to student life and the quality of undergraduate education.

Canadian universities insist that undergraduate teaching is a paramount mission at least equal to research as a priority. We maintain that instruction is now clearly secondary to research as a priority. Research drives all Canadian universities and all disciplines within them. Factions within the university, otherwise deeply divided, share the common denominator of research.

Over the past two decades, research has transformed Canadian universities. It has done so without reference to overarching educational or public policy principles, to the detriment of universities' quality and to the detriment of their overall contribution to Canadian society. Its costs and benefits, especially its adverse impact on undergraduate education, demand debate.

What is research and how do universities define it? What kinds of research are best done at universities? Should all universities undertake research in the same way? Such questions are seldom asked. We take them seriously and try to outline various meanings of university research. A clear theme emerges. Canadian universities undertake many scholarly activities. As J.A. Corry puts it: "The present-day university is a house of many mansions."[1] Sadly, the university's rich diversity is lost by its current emphasis on research that discovers new things, that adds information to the present stock, and that manifests itself in formal publication. Universities' embrace of a narrow, monolithic definition of research causes them to undervalue other scholarship, which while important to students and to society, is now deemed insignificant.

We compare the promise of university research with its practice in Canadian universities. We note major discrepancies between the promise and the reality, including heavy emphasis on the quantity of research, the development of an unfair status system within universities, and professorial misconduct. A significant problem is the increasingly specialized nature of much university research.

Admirers of universities often admit to such problems. But they see them as exceptions to the rule, as minor problems in a system of great accomplishment. Our view is that the problems are systemic, widespread, and inescapable in the university as now conceived.

Three other points merit attention. First, supporters of university research often dismiss critics as old-fashioned people who ignore or misunderstand change, technological progress, and economic advance. In their view, research critics want to shackle universities and thereby impede progress. We urge caution about this stereotype. Critics of university research hold various political and economic views. Abraham Flexner, for example, was a leading critic of research at large North American universities.[2] But he deeply admired the economic impact of research at German universities. His complaint about North American universities was that research was often trivial, incompetently undertaken, and without social significance. Similarly, J.A. Corry, the distinguished Queen's principal, was critical of contemporary ideas about university research.[3] He fully understood the economic significance of research and the need for a strong research base at universities. The point is clear. Critics of university research are seldom naive advocates of universities as ivory towers. On the contrary, they are intellectually and politically diverse, often aware of economic imperatives and rooted in several educational traditions.

Second, debate about university research is more sophisticated in the United States than in Canada. Thoughtful Americans have often criticized university research in principle and practice.[4] And they have been met by intelligent counterattacks. Canadians have never engaged the debate. Similarly, informed American opinion now openly acknowledges the sorry state of undergraduate education at American universities. It is no longer a debating point. As the Boyer Commission, a blue ribbon panel appointed by the major American research universities, argues: "We believe that the state of undergraduate education at research universities is such a crisis, an issue of such magnitude and volatility that universities must galvanize themselves to respond."[5] No Canadian university publicly admits to this view.

Third, we believe that university professors must engage in rigorous scholarly activities that yield publications and other forms of public display. We also believe, however, that professors must undertake reflective inquiry – the structured, painstaking examination of large questions from a variety of angles and over a long period. We do not believe that professors must constantly do research that generates new facts and that is immediately publishable.

THE DOMINANCE OF RESEARCH

Universities have defined themselves as Canada's central research institutions. This self-image rests on the idea that university research is unique in several ways. First, university research is allegedly free from vested interests. Second, it is said to be uniquely informed by its interaction with advanced teaching. Third, it is allegedly broader and richer than that undertaken by individuals and other institutions.

Canadian universities are motivated by the ideals of American research universities. As a result, they march to the beat of the same drummer. As Charles Anderson puts it: "Another reason it is so hard to get a perspective on the university is that the philosophy and structures, the procedures and the rituals, of the research university have largely become standard for the system. They are the universal model of all institutions of higher education. . . . The very universality of the model set by the research university tends to confirm its 'naturalness' and its legitimacy. To teach otherwise than is prescribed by the established organized disciplines seems vaguely suspect. It smacks of quackery."[6] In other words, the ideal of the American research university is so dominant that contrary views of the university are seen as radical. In the modern age, a university dedicated to teaching would immediately be labelled inferior, irrelevant, and unlikely to attract good students or professors.

In its annual survey of Canadian universities, *Maclean's* magazine adopts a threefold classification. Fifteen universities, including the University of Toronto, the University of British Columbia, and McGill, are designated as "Medical-Doctoral" universities. These institutions have a "broad range" of research and doctoral programs. They have Faculties of Medicine. A second group of thirteen, including York University, Simon Fraser University, and the University of New Brunswick, have diverse programs, lots of graduate studies, and considerable research. The third and largest group is "primarily undergraduate" universities. They (obviously) focus on undergraduate education. This group includes Acadia University, the University of Lethbridge, Bishop's University, and Laurentian University.

Some sense of scale and context is important when looking at these three groups. For example, any three universities in category I or II would probably have more undergraduate students than the twenty-three undergraduate universities combined. In other words, category I and II universities graft graduate students and advanced research on a large undergraduate base. They are multiversities as described in Chapter 2.

A *Maclean's* reader would likely assume that different universities see research in different ways. Surely Brock University in St. Catharines with 6,000 students has a different philosophy than York in suburban Toronto with almost 28,000 full-time students, let alone the University of Toronto with 50,000 students? But consider Brock's submission to the Commission of Inquiry on Canadian University Education: "Brock University also emphasizes excellence in research and scholarship for faculty members. There should ideally be a symbiosis between university education and faculty scholarship since faculty who are up-to-date in their respective fields are better prepared to teach effectively."[7]

Through these words, Brock places itself squarely in the North American orthodoxy. Its professors, to teach effectively, must be busy researchers. It simply has fewer students than York or the University of Toronto. Consider another example. Mount Saint Vincent University in Halifax was originally a Catholic women's college that is now a public university with 2,200 students. Surely such an institution would be out of the mainstream. On the contrary, in major decisions about promotion and tenure, Mount Saint Vincent sees teaching and research as equal in importance.

The grip of research can be seen in another way. Many Canadian universities were designed to be different. Three modern examples stand out: Carleton University, York University, and the University of Northern British Columbia (UNBC). Each was to fulfil a different role in the higher education system and to provide an alternative. Carleton was originally a night school whose teachings were aimed at civil servants and veterans in Ottawa after the Second World War. York University was seen as an alternative to the University of Toronto, whose arrogance and sense of tradition had become irritating. York was organized around colleges and offered night programs through Atkinson College and bilingual programs at Glendon College. University of Northern British Columbia in Prince George was to be student and community oriented. It was to be in tune with the needs of rugged, resource-based communities.

In each case, reforming zeal was quickly extinguished. Carleton rapidly became a "comprehensive" university that stressed research in social sciences. York's conversion to orthodoxy was rapid and complete. Its first president, Murray Ross, wrote about how York quickly moved from a desire to be different to a desire to be "better" in scholarship than its arch rival, University of Toronto.[8] Research, not a unique student experience, became York's hallmark. UNBC is on its way to orthodoxy. After less than a decade, its professors note a loss of distinctiveness.[9] The North American ideal of the professor – part teacher, part researcher – is the model. UNBC's faculty evaluation procedures, like those of other universities, stress research and publications.

Surely different disciplines harbour different ideas about research. How could a philosopher, a nuclear physicist, and a mechanical engineer all embrace a similar philosophy? The study and practice of higher education in North America provides a clear answer to this question. The ideals and research models of modern science have been adopted, albeit with modifications, by other disciplines.

The story is straightforward. After the Second World War, North American professors became impressed by, often envious of, the growing prestige of science and medicine, which were the darlings of governments and the object of public esteem. Unwilling to tolerate inferior status, social sciences imitated natural sciences, medicine, and engineering. They argued that their research was relevant and socially significant. They too would have doctoral and graduate programs that linked professors with specialized graduate students. They would not be relegated to the task of teaching undergraduate students while scientists did research and received public acclaim.

Professors of radically different political and ideological views share similar views about research. For example, Marxist economists are as committed to research and publication as are doctrinaire free-market economists and theoretical mathematical economists. Feminists have attacked male dominance of modern universities. They lament women's underrepresentation in faculty positions and senior administrative posts and the lack of concern with women's issues in the curriculum and in textbooks. That said, feminist scholars embrace conventional ideas about university research. They simply want more research *by* women and *about* women.

A more complex issue is the growth of new ideas about knowledge and power in society variously called postmodernism, radical relativism, and, even more loosely, political correctness.[10] Such schools of thought reject the idea that there are truths in the universe that can be objectively determined. On the contrary, our understandings of the world are said to be politically determined, subject to multiple interpretations, and, ultimately, expressions of prevailing power structures.

Such views open up countless questions. Is the university simply a conduit for oppressive views about capitalism, gender, and social class? What does it mean to say that literature and music are expressions of power? What is medical science about from this vantage point? Should the university give "voice" to women, Aboriginal peoples, persons of colour, and gays?

Postmodern ideas have had little impact in the natural sciences, engineering, economics, psychology, and medicine, where conventional ideas about truth and research prevail. Faculties of Business, Law, and Physical Education and areas such as political science, philosophy, history, and sociology all have some adherents, but they remain the minority. Postmodernists reign in departments such as English, comparative literature, and women's studies and in fields such as film studies and cultural studies. They are powerful in Faculties of Education.

Postmodernism adds a new divide between professors and between professors and students. It has also expanded the range of issues that universities define as worthy of teaching and research. Depending on one's views, the new areas are creative and stimulating or offensive and trivial. Under postmodernism, no subject is inherently more important than any other. Hence no topic is beyond a professor's legitimate interest. Such things as the culture of shopping centres and the social significance of Madonna and the World Wrestling Federation are all worthy of study.

Postmodernism also generates its own form of interdisciplinary studies. Since every societal phenomenon is somehow an expression of power, an English professor sees himself as fully qualified to analyze the politics of literature. Postmodern philosophers examine subjects that normally preoccupy sociologists. Sociologists probe painting, music, professional sports, and literature.

Yet postmodernists are fully professionalized university researchers who operate within North American orthodoxy. Their work, like all modern university scholarship, is highly specialized. Certain strands of postmodern thought are renowned for theoretical abstraction. It has its own specialized language. Postmodernists "interrogate" subjects and are heavily engaged in "deconstruction" and "discourse analysis." Like all university professors, they publish extensively, operate networks of journals and conferences, and expect government funding for their research. Postmodernists accept the obligation of professors to do research and the existence of a "superstar" status system among professors and between universities. Postmodernists have not contributed creative, let alone radical, ideas to debates about the relationship between teaching and research, about research ethics, or about university governance.

IMPACTS OF RESEARCH

Americans have long acknowledged that professorial research has caused undergraduate teaching to decline as a university priority. As the Boyer report on undergraduate teaching at American research universities puts it: "Advanced research and undergraduate teaching have existed on two quite different planes, the first a source of pleasure, recognition and reward, the latter a burden shouldered more or less reluctantly to maintain the viability of the institution."[11]

An academic revolution transformed intellectual life in the twentieth century.[12] After the Second World War, North American professors were transformed from thinkers into specialized experts. Scholarship was organized into increasingly independent disciplines. Aspiring members of disciplines were trained in research techniques in doctoral programs in research universities. Professors became driven by disciplinary norms and by the needs of a small number of graduate students. However, professors worked within universities that also taught large numbers of undergraduate students. No university could sustain battalions of expert professors without large undergraduate programs beneath them.

A vicious circle thus emerged in North American universities. Specialized research professors were obliged to teach undergraduates. By definition, undergraduate teaching was hard work. Professors' true love was the library or the laboratory, certainly not the lecture hall. The students, who want broad knowledge, wrongly assumed that professors are devoted to teaching full time.

Writing in 1936, Robert Hutchins, then president of the University of Chicago, observed how the doctoral degree in American universities was a research degree whose content and philosophy was indifferent to teaching. As Hutchins puts it: "The students who are going to be teachers are put through a procedure which was designed to produce investigators."[13] Writing in 1997, Donald Kennedy, a former president of Stanford University, echoed Hutchins' point.[14] New Stanford professors in the 1990s, the recent graduates of the doctoral programs, came with little enthusiasm or background preparation for their onerous roles as teachers. They were ill-prepared for the classroom and often disinterested in professorial duties such as counselling students, thinking carefully about teaching, and devising creative courses.

So what if Americans think undergraduate programs at their universities are poor? Is Canada different? Does undergraduate teaching really have lower status than research in Canadian universities? Consider the following facts.

In the course of our research, we interviewed more than thirty faculty members in seven universities in four provinces. Our interviewees included young professors and professors nearing retirement, men and women who were members of more than a dozen disciplines including electrical engineering, physics, and various branches of medical science. Not one professor believed that teaching was more important than research at his or her university. And while all Canadian universities profess to weight teaching and research equally, only a handful even thought that their university honoured this formal commitment when hiring and undertaking promotions. A large majority claimed that research was given much more weight than teaching and that the imbalance was growing greater.[15]

Canadian universities have often complained about the erosion of the university research infrastructure during the 1990s. By this they mean the deterioration and growing obsolescence of buildings, laboratory equipment, computing services, and libraries. That said, few Canadian universities have defined better common space, better classrooms, and better library facilities for undergraduate students as an essential priority.

To our knowledge, no Canadian university in recent memory has hired a senior professor from another university because of his or her demonstrated teaching skills. Research drives the job market, a fact not lost on Canadian professors. Nor is demonstrated competence as an undergraduate teacher a requirement for appointment to senior administrative positions in Canadian universities, notably the presidency.

Vast amounts of undergraduate teaching are done by part-time, sessional staff. This allows tenured professors to do more specialized teaching and more research. Canadian universities *never* hire part-time or sessional staff to do important research projects. Canadian universities envision study leave, sabbaticals as they are sometimes called, as research leave. The professor's obligation is to undertake a research project.

Canadian university professors with tenure can reduce their teaching load in various ways. Teaching can be reduced by administrative service, by receipt of research grants that provide funds to "buy" course "relief" from the university, and by negotiation with outside organizations to buy out teaching time so that more research can be done. In a recent policy initiative, the Social Sciences and Humanities Research Council of Canada provided universities with funds that allow young professors to buy out their teaching. The program is designed to provide young professors time, not to do research but to prepare research grant proposals.

Until recently, Canadian universities sought the opinion of professors at other universities only when considering applicants for promotion to the rank of professor, the highest rank. Now most universities seek external assessors for the tenure decision and the decision to promote to associate professor, the intermediate professorial rank. As we note in Chapter 3, such a practice stresses research by design. It places great weight on the opinions of external professors who know only the published research and who know nothing firsthand about teaching quality. This practice decisively and consciously tips the balance toward research in key university decisions about tenure and promotion.

Research causes universities to distinguish themselves on the basis of prestige not accomplishment. The number of renowned researchers on campus and the amount of external funding for research are deemed indicators of university prestige. In a worrisome way, prestige becomes synonymous with educational quality. As Jacques Barzun puts it: "Greatness and a glorious reputation descended on institutions after a long course of remarkable achievements. Prestige is preposterous, i.e., it is acquired first instead of arriving last. Prestige means choosing faculty appointees who will look stunning in the press release. Prestige means getting the man or the line of goods that has just come into prominence ... Prestige means getting a good rating in the surveys and polls of excellence, and avoiding trouble so as to appear in the press both frequently and favorably."[16]

Universities' commitment to research has brought them into close relationships with governments that fund it. Research thus gives governments influence over university priorities. In Canada, four federal government agencies – the Canadian Institutes of Health Research (formerly the Medical Research Council of Canada), the Natural Sciences and Engineering Research Council of Canada (NSERCC), the Social Science and Humanities Research Council of Canada (SSHRCC), and the Canada Foundation for Innovation (CFI) – are influential in the councils of universities.

Federal research agencies shape professors' research agendas. Their influence is inescapable insofar as professorial careers, especially in science and medicine, are heavily determined by success in obtaining grants. The granting councils establish guidelines about ethics, the employment of researchers, students, and technicians that shape university priorities.

More important, the federal research councils pay only the direct costs of research. The operating costs of buildings, wear and tear on university laboratories and other elements of overhead, are borne by universities. In a telling way, universities, by complaining about the overhead problem, acknowledge that research imposes substantial costs on them and that undergraduate teaching suffers as a result.

The work done for the granting councils – applying for grants, adjudicating applications, developing policy – consumes tremendous professorial time. Universities sponsor seminars about how to gain research grants. They employ administrative staffs to take care of accounting and related matters. University administrators must worry about cuts in funding for research. As Clark Kerr said of the postwar American scene, the federal granting agencies are the universities' new alma mater.[17]

THE MEANING OF RESEARCH

What is research, the activity that dominates Canadian universities and that is now the obligation of all professors? This question is more readily asked than answered. Research is an omnipresent activity that is certainly not a university monopoly. We do research when we shop. The research is sometimes complex when a major purchase is involved. It is routine for common products such as bread, colas, and vegetables. To take another example, professional baseball relies heavily on "research." Outstanding hitters, pitchers, and managers are often renowned "students" who study statistical data about the performance of their opponents. High school students routinely do research papers. All sorts of adjectives precede the noun "research." We have consumer research, basic research, applied research, fashion research, and labour market research, to cite a few examples. Corporations, trade unions, and governments all do research. What therefore is unique about university research?

Modern university research is principally about the "discovery" of new insights into the human condition in all its aspects. This sort of research is labelled "frontier research" by Louis-Philippe Bonneau and J.A. Corry. It is also called "original research."[18] Frontier research at the university conjures up images of inquiry that leads to new understandings of ourselves, medical breakthroughs, and a deeper understanding of science. The researcher is constantly working at the cutting edge, and as Bonneau and Corry's term implies, pushing back the frontiers of knowledge. Discovery, not reflection, is the heart of university research.

All parts of the university pursue "new" knowledge. Medical science does research that leads to new drugs and new treatments. Economists and sociologists generate data about economic and social conditions. Astronomers scan the skies for new galaxies, stars, and moons. Even philosophers and English professors see their role as opening new vistas in literature.

In his critique of higher education, Robert Hutchins maintains that university research rests on simplistic ideas about society and progress. Frontier research was often simply fact gathering: "The more information, the more discoveries, the more inventions, the more progress. The way to promote progress was therefore to get more information."[19] His view was that fact finding, while important, should seldom be done at a university, which by definition pursues deeper matters.

Hutchins highlights the deeper views of understanding and human progress that underpin frontier research. Knowledge in the research university is produced by the daily research of the professors and to a lesser degree the students. The idea is that each "knowledge producer" explores a fragment of the intellectual universe. Her minute contribution is put in context with all others that have researched before her. As each scholar produces a tiny brick of information, the larger skyscraper of human understanding is thought to arise. The modern professor, far from being a person of extraordinary intellect and broad insight, is a highly specialized tradesperson in the knowledge factory. As Charles Anderson puts it: "But now the task of the university is to manufacture knowledge, and the work is understood to be a collaborative undertaking, not a solitary affair. Great visions are rare and progress comes by small steps. Understanding emerges gradually through intricate, specialized organization and teamwork."[20]

Modern university research, to be legitimate in professors' eyes, must be published. Hence "publish or perish" is the motto of modern universities. Teaching students is no longer seen as an adequate means of the dissemination of knowledge. The publication of research in books and scholarly articles is now an imperative. Publication rests on the assumption that published, professorial research is synonymous with knowledge.

Publication has many dimensions in Canadian universities. First, "real" research is peer reviewed before publication. Peers are other members of the academic profession, be it political science, botany, or cardiology. The peers must assess the research, verify that it is technically correct, examine its relationship to the published literature, and establish that it makes a contribution to knowledge. Without peer approval, research is often deemed neither publishable nor valuable.

Peer review has a hallowed position in the modern university. It is thought to be fair, objectively undertaken in most instances, and essential to academic freedom. The notions that nonspecialists should be allowed to assess university research or that its general relevance, as opposed to its technical merit, should be examined are outrageous to the vast majority of university professors. A powerful indictment of a professor is that she has not published in peer-reviewed outlets.

Different outlets for research are not of equal value. Professors must place their research in prestigious venues. As we note in Chapter 3, each discipline has a hierarchy of learned journals and publishers. To be published in a top-ranked journal (the ranking is done by members of the academic profession) is the goal of most Canadian professors. The dubious assumption is that the more prestigious the outlet, the greater the wisdom imparted by the writing. Underpinning this notion are other questionable assumptions, including that the more prestigious journals and book publishers have wiser editors, better peer reviewers, and greater independence from the intellectual fads. When universities assess professors for promotion and merit pay, they often judge the quality of research simply by examining its venues. Often the work is not read. Publication in a good venue is often proof enough of quality and significance.

Canadian universities undervalue another powerful form of research best called reflective inquiry.[21] Reflective inquiry is a complex activity with several characteristics. First, it involves careful thought about the human condition. Second, reflective inquiry involves disciplined thinking about scholarship beyond one's own specialization and discipline. It is an inherently interdisciplinary activity. Reflective inquiry demands rigorous thought about what we know, or claim to know; the underlying assumptions; and the key questions for inquiry. In this sense, it can be conceived as research about research. Third, it involves assessments of the underlying principles and ideas in one's own scholarship and discipline. Fourth, reflective inquiry must put present understandings in context with past ones. Finally, reflective inquiry involves constant assessment of one's own strengths and weaknesses as a scholar. These various dimensions of reflective inquiry are summarized in the words of Louis-Philippe Bonneau and J.A. Corry: "We are no longer putting Nature on the rack to be interrogated: we are conducting an inquiry into thought, examining the principles and theories by which the sum of our knowledge, whether in a narrow sector, a wide sector, or over the whole range, has been given coherence and meaning; we are looking perhaps for a new projection for the map of knowledge ... We are reflecting on what is conceivably knowable, on hypotheses about man and his world."[22]

An example of reflective inquiry would be a careful study of the continued relevance of federalism as a form of democratic government for Canada. Such an analysis would necessarily ask, By what principles should Canadians govern themselves? How much social diversity does federalism demand (or generate)? What sorts of political conflicts are best resolved by federal forms of government? Such a reflective inquiry would go far beyond the conventional boundaries of political science to embrace the contributions of lawyers, sociologists, and economists, to name just a few. It would carefully probe the conventional wisdom about federalism. And it would discern and explain major neglected questions. The best frontier researchers are (or should be) interested in such foundational questions. But their studies take the status quo for granted and seldom probe larger questions. Their purpose is to generate insights into specific characteristics of Canadian federalism. Do Albertans differ from Nova Scotians and Manitobans in their views about political authority? Has the Millennium Scholarship program generated intergovernmental conflict? How is health care restructuring in Ontario influenced by federal decisions?

Distinctions between frontier research and reflective inquiry are not always precise. But several essential things can be said safely. First, few thinkers, let alone university professors, master both major types of re-search. John Maynard Keynes, Charles Darwin, and Sigmund Freud are among the very few who have successfully pushed back the frontiers of understanding *and* reflected deeply about existing understandings of society. Second, the first point notwithstanding, many professors challenge the distinction between frontier research and reflective inquiry. They see themselves as contributing to both and, hence, see the distinction as false. But when pressed, professors simply claim that their current research, while narrow and empirical, is reflective inquiry because it is remotely linked to broader issues. This common argument does not hold water. For example, large cities are central features of modern society. But a professor who undertakes a painstaking study of the social backgrounds of Canadian mayors is not, contrary to his claims, undertaking reflective inquiry simply because he sheds a tiny ray of light on urban government. His study neither asks nor illuminates the deeper questions that reflective inquiry demands.

Reflective inquiry may be a solitary pastime but it need not be. It can take various forms, including vigorous discussions with colleagues and arguments with students. It can and should lead to publication of various sorts. It will invariably make informed contributions to undergraduate teaching, where the premium is on broad, informed reading not specialized publication. If done at a high level, reflective inquiry will certainly inform the best frontier research.

Canadian universities are becoming indifferent to reflective inquiry. Con-templative scholars and teachers are no longer admired (unless they also publish major works or make impressive discoveries continuously). They are seen as deadwood whose contribution is minor compared with special-ists who busily write papers about narrow topics. Students need exposure to both types of research and professors need to understand and respect both types of research. Serious frontier researchers must understand, if not paint, the broader picture. The reflective scholar must examine, understand, and at least occasionally do original research. Otherwise scholarship and teaching become stale, removed from human reality, and uninspiring to students. Few professors will excel at both types of research. Universities must embrace both within their walls.

Beyond frontier research and reflective inquiry, university professors do many other kinds of research. Important research that improves teaching is ignored. How could wide reading and thought about how to teach a large class of second-year students the Canadian constitution be considered serious research when it is not published?

Another example is limited university respect for authors of textbooks. The thoughtful preparation of undergraduate textbooks is an exhausting process that demands broad understanding. It needs a clarity of prose and expression not required when writing for professional colleagues. It requires reflection about a vital question – what do students, the vast majority of whom will not be university professors – need to know about chemistry, economics, or philosophy? The content and power of a textbook can shape many more lives than countless specialized articles. Canadian universities heap no esteem on textbook writers.[23] For they are merely reviewing what others have said. They are not contributing new findings, which is allegedly what real research is about.

Hours of thought and general reading that underpin presentations to parliamentary committees, community groups, and high school classes are not considered research either. The ability to make complex concepts understandable to nonuniversity audiences requires considerable self-discipline, broad learning, and a grasp of basics. But such activities are sometimes viewed with disdain and indifference by colleagues. Professorial work that advances strong arguments about "real world" issues is seldom regarded as important university research. For it might not be peer reviewed and, hence, technically proficient. It is more of a pastime, a hobby, than serious scholarship. Professors with high profiles and esteem in society are often seen as second-rate researchers who can't cut it in the world of professional scholarship.

Such attitudes, while damaging to the university, are not surprising. They are the predictable views of modern university professors who define themselves as members of specialized disciplines. Canadian professors relate principally to other professors who share common disciplinary perspectives. They want the respect of professional peers, not of students or the society at large. Their currency is the number of specialized publications they produce and the professional esteem that flows from those articles. An acknowledged presence on the cutting edge is their ambition.

UNIVERSITY RESEARCH: PROMISE AND REALITY

Canadian universities claim that their research is the source of advances in health sciences, a deeper understanding of social conditions, and an expanding economy. An alternative to this view is to see the university as a knowledge factory dedicated to the production of research. The image of a knowledge factory is a powerful one. It demystifies university research and advances images of bureaucratized processes, not spontaneous, creative ones.

University Research: Quantity or Quality?
University ideals demand that research be thoughtfully conceived and of high quality. This ideal is abused in Canadian universities where the quantity of research is used to evaluate individual professors, departments, and even whole universities.

The vocabulary of university professors betrays their emphasis on the quantity of research. Faculty members speak constantly about research productivity. As August comes to an end and students prepare to return to campus, professors worry about their research output over the summer. Particularly worrisome are rumours that a professor plumbing the same depths has been churning it out in recent months. In a related vein, professors, when asked hard questions, almost invariably say: "More research will have to be done before I can respond." In other words, if enough bricks are laid, the mansion will rise.

Universities justify their heavy emphasis on quantity of research publication on two unimpressive grounds. First, quantitative measures are required because it is allegedly hard to judge the quality of research and to evaluate its impact over time. Thus universities simply count published pages. Twenty pages are twice as good as ten. Second, research is now so specialized that it cannot really be evaluated by colleagues even in the same discipline or department. While probably true in many instances, this argument is itself a damning indictment of modern university research.

Consider the following commentary by Jacques Barzun about university research: "One has only to listen to the private confidences of the ablest scientists and scholars, and to have some familiarity with a given subject to be persuaded that an enormous amount of the research output in all fields is: (1) repetition in swollen fragments of what was known more compactly and elegantly before; (2) repetition, conscious or not, of new knowledge found by others; (3) repetition of oneself in diverse forms; (4) original worthlessness."[24] Canadian universities cannot easily refute Barzun's comments. For to do so would hammer at their foundations. How can a university, committed to original thinking and to the view that each professor must do research, admit that research is often repetitive?

Commentators often assert that modern society is undergoing a knowledge explosion. The world is changing rapidly, they opine, as inventions proliferate and as knowledge becomes dated. It is often said that more research is needed if we are to keep pace. But the very notion of a knowledge explosion is partly created by current ideas about university research. Remember the basic elements of university thinking: Every professor must be a frontier researcher. Every piece of frontier research is knowledge. University professors are obliged to do research. More and more research is being done at universities so, given prevailing definitions, knowledge is always being created.

Research Specialization

University research is very specialized. Throughout the twentieth century, fields and subfields have proliferated. The resulting university is intellectually fragmented. The process of specialization is relentless and self-sustaining. Even in political science, a simple field compared with microbiology, specialization is rampant. Experts on particular countries argue that their research is unique. They need their own journals, their own conferences, and their own research programs. Twenty years ago, a Canadian politics professor might note "comparative constitutions," that is, an interest in the constitutional traditions of other countries, as a specialization. Canadian politics professors now define themselves as experts on particular sections of the Canadian Charter of Rights and Freedoms.

Universities have not thought deeply about rampant specialization, although they have sometimes considered the quite different question of whether every university needs to teach in every area. Specialization has generally been seen as an inevitable and generally benign process. Greater specialization is a fact of modern life, a sign of societal sophistication and progress. Alternatively, specialization is lamented but nothing is done.

Universities are too tolerant of scholarly specialization. They have not asked hard questions about its necessity, about its consequences for the university, or about its impact on teaching. To our way of thinking, specialization has two serious consequences. First, as research becomes more specialized, the big picture becomes more obscure. Researchers, far from looking at society as a whole, operate within their disciplines and its narrow boundaries. Professors, hard at specialized frontier research, seldom reflect. They often read little beyond their own subdiscipline, let alone in other disciplines. And this gives rise to the point, frequently made in the United States, that university research has limited influence on public policy. General interpretations of society are often done by thinkers who are not university based.

A second consequence of research specialization is its spillover into undergraduate teaching. Americans have often noted that professors teach less and less over time in major American universities. But at the same time, departments offer more courses, especially at the senior undergraduate (third- and fourth-year) and graduate levels. This is so because professors now offer undergraduate courses in their fields of research expertise.

This bad trend is a triumph of professorial preferences and research over the educational needs of students. Specialized courses may well be interesting, popular among students, and enthusiastically delivered. But their inclusion in the university curriculum is based solely on the fact that professors find the subject personally interesting. No careful thought is given to the long-term needs of students, to the relationship between general and specialized courses, or to a general philosophy of education.

Power and Status Differentials

The modern professor is an independent fundraiser.[25] She presents research proposals to granting agencies, which in turn award funds directly to successful professors. Armed with large grants, the recipient professor, however modest her intellect, has power. She has a capacity to hire graduate students, to shape their research priorities, and to influence department priorities. The grant-winning professor is sought after by deans and vice-presidents for advice on university policy. The well-funded professor sits on committees that establish priorities for granting councils and so on. The successful frontier researcher sometimes becomes unruly and hard to manage, like a thoroughbred on a rich pre-race diet.[26] But there is seldom anything intrinsically meritorious or superior about well-funded research projects or research professors.

Two decades ago the serious reflective professor was still a revered figure on North American university campuses. His breadth of knowledge, his power of expression, and his love of learning were widely admired.[27] In the new millennium, professors dedicated to broad and deep thinking are often in conflict with the dominant frontier researchers. The gap between the two sorts of professors is profound. The frontier researcher sees the reflective inquirer as unproductive, lazy, and unworthy of professorial status. Why should someone sit around reading and thinking while I knock myself out getting grants, writing papers, and attending conferences? As the critics often say, the reflective inquirer gets a full salary for half the job. He is not regularly producing articles, books, or experiments so by definition he is not really working. This tension also manifests in ideas about teaching. The frontier researcher argues that the reflective inquirer exaggerates the rigours of undergraduate teaching. For the frontier researcher, a "solid" course gets decent student ratings and is reworked once every five or seven years. Teaching is a straightforward, mechanical matter.

Universities certainly harbour legitimate intellectual leaders. This is not surprising given the view that knowledge emerges slowly, with each professor contributing a tiny piece to the larger edifice. In the knowledge factory, some workers will be able to build larger pieces more quickly than their peers. And sometimes they have a clear vision of how the different pieces are coming together and what the resulting structure will look like. Such intellectual leaders embody authority of competence and merit esteem.

But many academic superstars are not much different from other professors. They are often more lucky than able. Sometimes scholars labour in obscurity until government granting agencies define their research as strategically important. Suddenly the obscure professor is on the cutting edge. But he need not be particularly meritorious or even smart. In academic life as in Hollywood, reputation is often as much manufactured as earned. Ambitious frontier researchers cultivate contacts, skilfully select conferences for self-promotion, and court favour with university leaders. This matters because productive researchers are generally paid more and teach less. Their opinions will be widely sought as will their services by competing universities. Moreover, research acumen is the sole basis of superstar status. The outstanding undergraduate teacher is rewarded only through the respect of his students and, at best, the grudging tolerance of colleagues.

Research drives a wedge between scholars in different departments. Science, medicine, and engineering enjoy substantial respect in the community at large. Their research exerts impact on national well-being. Other faculties and disciplines have rejected their role as second fiddles. They have met the challenge of science with a strategy of imitation. Areas like fine arts, English, and philosophy expend enormous energy in raising their status within the university and the society. Their strategy is to argue that their research is as important as that of science and medicine. This "me too" strategy comes at the expense of serious teaching, a strength that is much more natural and politically powerful for a Faculty of Arts.

Wasted Effort

Canadian universities tolerate professorial games whose sole purpose is to gain research grants and recognition. In fact, the academic entrepreneur, the busy professor who knows how to play the game, is often admired on campus. Such behaviour mocks scholarly ideals about research as part of a quest for truth and deeper understanding.

Canadian professors waste energy in activities designed to increase the quantity of scholarly papers produced. The most common strategy – conscious repetition – has been noted. Professors write essentially the same paper for various outlets and purposes. Modern word processors facilitate repetition. Large sections of manuscripts can easily be incorporated into "new" work. Driven by disciplines and by university rules about promotion, professors knowingly tolerate repetition, or "recycling" as the practice is called. Sometimes the repetition is deliberate. At other times, the professor working in a tiny corner sees a minor new point as a major discovery worthy of new papers. He bristles at the notion that he is tedious.

Professors increasingly work in teams that divide research more minutely so that more of it can be done and published. An assembly line is thus created. Teams are driven by the logic of increasing output, not understanding. Graduate students are recruited so that the team can be larger, more specialized, and hence more productive. Work is often driven by arbitrary deadlines, a fact that insults intellectual principles. It is also done more quickly than it should be. Hasty work is done primarily because of prevailing ideas about productivity. It results from university timelines about promotion and salaries. For example, in universities with annual merit pay systems, professors devise strategies to publish large amounts within each calendar year so as to maximize their salaries. The early stages of a scholarly career lay the foundations for subsequent behaviour. As Chapter 3 shows, professors seeking tenure formulate plans, with the advice of senior colleagues who know the game, to ensure that enough papers are produced. They are on the treadmill early.

Professors devise teaching schedules that maximize their research time. Common strategies are teaching only on certain days of the week so that research and travel time are increased and readily planned. Teaching is often limited to formal classroom activity and the minimum required after-class contact with students. Professors avoid large courses for beginning students and new courses that are not related to their research interests. Professors with large research grants have superior resources and incentives to participate in such activities. They "buy out" their teaching time. This practice gives others the incentive to get grants so that they too can get out of teaching and compete on a level playing field with their colleagues. A vicious circle emerges. Universities seldom question the underlying premise – that professors' research should drive the content, timing, and nature of the undergraduate students' education. Why is the priority not reversed?

An industry revolves around the pursuit of research grants. The term grantsmanship refers to the tactics used to get research grants. Universities are not shy about these activities. They hold seminars where professors gather to hear the ways of the successful professors. Professors anticipate the views of the adjudicating panels, learn buzzwords, and construct their resumes so that their research track record is put in the best possible light. Research teams are constructed with more care and political consideration than a cabinet being planned by a prime minister. The content of research – what is studied and by whom – is unquestionably shaped by this competition.

Universities even put in place funding programs for the unsuccessful applicants so that they can proceed a bit further with their studies before reapplication. Lengthy post mortems occur about what went right and wrong and what remedial work is required. Enormous amounts of university resources are expended. As Page Smith says of the modern university research: "It is busy work on a vast, almost incomprehensible scale."[28]

Undergraduate students have become afterthoughts in universities. The content and timing of courses and the designation of instructors is principally driven by the research interests of the professors. University tolerance of assembly-line, hastily produced research debases scholarly ideals that stress rigour, deep thought, and long-term thinking. Strategies to get grants, to increase research output, and to avoid undergraduate students show disdain for students, for scholarship, and for the public that foots the bills. Ambitious professors eager to build their research profile are allowed, often encouraged, to offload large classes, administrative work, and serious student counselling.

Unethical Conduct

University research is sometimes plagued by unethical conduct. Among the activities are conscious falsification of research results, theft of others' work, and the suppression of research results for nonscholarly reasons. Conflicts of interest occur when professors have commercial and financial interests in the results of their research.[29] Such misconduct is explored in greater detail in Chapter 7.

Little serious discussion has occurred in Canada about unethical behaviour at universities. University leaders imply that all organizations have a few bad apples or, alternatively, that decent people sometimes become overzealous. In their view, some misconduct is inevitable even if reprehensible. It is certainly not a large enough problem to cause serious reflection about university research.

Most unethical conduct rooted in the nature of modern university research is structural, not simply a reflection of personal failings. One obvious cause of misconduct is the commercialization of research, a subject explored in Chapter 8. Some university research is now often driven by commercial considerations, as manifest by partnerships involving universities, firms, and researchers in the pursuit of new products and processes. Fields such as computer science, molecular biology, and various branches of agriculture are now problematic for universities because of large potential profit from scientific breakthroughs in these areas.[30]

Commercial university research is certainly not the exclusive cause of research misconduct. Falsification of data, plagiarism, and conflicts of interest are found in many areas of research that are not commercialized. In these areas, unethical conduct results from the overly competitive nature of research and the heavy weight placed by universities on research as a criterion of success. Pressures to publish, to be on the cutting edge, and to be internationally respected are intense in some quarters. The organization of some university research into large teams heightens competition and creates problems of weighting contribution and assigning credit.

CONCLUSION

Over the last thirty years, Canadian universities have adopted research as their principal role. Research shapes all Canadian universities. Research is an obligation of Canadian professors regardless of their discipline, aptitude, or inclination.

Professors have embraced their new role vigorously. Regardless of their political and ideological views or their gender, professors see research leading to publication as a mission. Even those who espouse a postmodern view embrace research.

A narrow view of research dominates Canadian universities. Professors seldom engage in reflective inquiry, by which we mean deep reflection about major issues. Instead they are driven by the ideal of frontier research, which values new findings. Considerable attention is paid to published articles, the audience of which is narrow specialists.

Research is now much more important than teaching in Canadian universities. Research accomplishment or potential is the crucial factor in university decisions about hiring, promotion, merit pay, and tenure. Curriculum is increasingly shaped by the research interests of professors rather than by careful examination of society's needs or by reflection about what students should know.

The dominant view, that each professor is a researcher and a teacher, extracts a toll. Undergraduate education suffers. Professors see research and graduate education as their keys to advancement. Undergraduate students, by far the numerically dominant force, are the lowest university priority.

Universities claim that this situation is somehow the fault of governments. On the contrary, it is the conscious choice of universities themselves.

Research leads to abuses of university ideals. Accomplished research professors are accorded unwarranted status. For no good reason, universities are competitive, stressful places. Moreover, the quality and relevance of research is seldom probed. Professors waste energy on strategies to maximize research output, to minimize contact with students, and to advance their careers through research.

Writing in 1936, Robert Hutchins, then president of the University of Chicago, foresaw and lamented the rise of research.[31] He thought that universities were trivialized by the forces of economic and scientific advancement. They were unwilling to resist calls for practical training and relevant research. Hutchins believed, as we do, that serious universities and all serious professors must do research. But he saw research as thoughtful consideration of major questions.

Contemporary apostles of the multiversity label Hutchins an elitist. But such a view is superficial. He saw applied scientific research, engineering, and practical social science as essential to human well-being. But he did not necessarily see them as university activities. Hutchins' theme is simple: Research embraces diverse activities, and certain sorts of research do not require university participation.

CHAPTER 6

TEACHING AND RESEARCH AT CANADIAN UNIVERSITIES

The Myth of Mutual Enrichment

Canadian universities vigorously assert that their teaching and research reinforce each other. They claim that university teaching is made lively and relevant when conducted by professors who are active researchers. Occasionally, universities also maintain that serious undergraduate teaching informs professorial research in ways that improve its quality and significance. Taken together, these two ideas comprise the mutual enrichment theory of university education. The essence of this revered concept is captured by Joseph Ben David: "The location of advanced research in independent and competing universities, in each of which there has been a constant flow of new researchers, has served effectively to enforce high intellectual standards, to recognize originality and to ensure the circulation of ideas to students, and through them to society at large. Severance of the connection between research and teaching would eliminate these highly desirable incentives to both intellectual and cultural vitality."[1]

The idea that teaching is improved by interaction with research is a foundational concept in Canadian universities. Among other things, the mutual enrichment notion is used to distinguish universities from other educational institutions. As professors often declare, research universities differ from colleges and technical institutes in that they conduct research that inspires teaching. The idea of mutual enrichment is also employed to differentiate modern research universities from their predecessors.

Research universities are depicted as vigorous places where cutting-edge research sustains and bolsters teaching. Great teachers are dynamic researchers whose classes come to life as they review their latest findings. The contrast is the dreary university of yesteryear where teaching was the dominant activity and where professors, who were not obliged to do research, transmitted established wisdom.

The theory of mutual enrichment performs important political functions in universities. It justifies the commitment of university resources to research. How can research be criticized when it simultaneously advances the well-being of society, the economy, and students? Mutual enrichment also provides some unity to fractious campuses. Botanists, academic lawyers, electrical engineers, and linguists have few common bonds. They share, however, the ideals that university research and teaching beneficially reinforce each other and that effective teachers are active researchers. Finally, mutual enrichment is an aspect of professors' drive for social status and influence. It is an idea that makes professors seem talented and multiskilled.

This chapter explores the mutual enrichment thesis in Canadian universities. It examines two major analyses of Canadian universities in 1991: the analysis by the Royal Society of Canada of the role of research in Canadian universities and the Smith Report commissioned by the Association of Universities and Colleges of Canada. The Royal Society's report is the modern professor's dream. It sees research as a university priority and a national imperative. Canadian universities, to be world class, required more government money to strengthen research and to develop elite researchers. Stuart Smith's report, widely anticipated to be a ringing endorsement of Canadian universities, became a university problem. Smith shocked universities when he challenged the mutual enrichment thesis, criticized research, and recommended that universities teach more and do a better job of it.

The Smith and Royal Society reports bear close scrutiny for several reasons. First, they present contrasting views about the role, importance, and obligations of Canadian universities. The Royal Society report is a coherent account, indeed the political manifesto, of the "new" Canadian university dedicated to world-class research, excellence in its endeavours, and the pursuit of national recognition. For his part, Smith saw universities in much more modest terms. Second, the two reports set the stage for much subsequent debate about Canadian universities. Finally, universities' rejection of Smith's call for better teaching reveal a lot about their priorities.

We explore arguments about the mutual enrichment thesis by noting two things. First, serious research does not sustain the mutual enrichment hypothesis. Second, conventional arguments in support of mutual enrichment are shown to be weak and lacking in evidence. At best, they are claims about a university world that ought to be.

Finally, the chapter examines the political functions of the mutual enrichment hypothesis and its future as a foundational concept. In particular, it examines why Canadian universities attacked the Smith Report. Our answer is that the mutual enrichment thesis is not really about educational principles. On the contrary, mutual enrichment is employed to make professors seem more important than "mere" teachers.

We note how research universities in the United States now openly acknowledge the flaws of the mutual enrichment doctrine. They now argue that efforts must be made to better connect teaching with research. In other words, links between teaching and research, which are supposed to occur naturally but have not, will be made to happen by university policy. We applaud this revolution in American thinking but worry about several specific reforms that it has spawned.

CONTRASTING VIEWS OF
TEACHING AND RESEARCH

In 1991, the Royal Society of Canada, a body of distinguished professors, issued its report entitled *Realizing the Potential: A Strategy for University Research in Canada*. The report signalled a new, exalted conception of the Canadian university.[2] For the Royal Society, research was the essence of a modern society's vitality, the university was a central research institution, and professors, particularly distinguished ones, were people of national consequence. Governments were urged to increase research funding so that Canada could develop elite researchers.

The Royal Society's report reflects the anxieties and ambitions of Canadian universities in a period of economic and social change. It is remarkably uncritical of universities and enormously self-confident in its intellectual correctness. Without reflection on alternatives or careful analysis, the Royal

Society announced research as the university's primary function. The Canadian public interest would be served by the creation, through public policy measures and increased government spending, of a cadre of elite researchers. The training of future researchers, heretofore an implicit role of universities, became a priority. The vast majority of university students, who would never become researchers let alone professors, were seen as potential recruits to the research cause. They were to leave the university respectful of the importance of research.

The Royal Society caught the spirit of the times when it asserted that Canadian university researchers must compete at the highest level of international research. It spoke an ideology of excellence. As the Royal Society put it: "Clearly the research environment of an advanced country such as Canada must make it possible for its outstanding scholars to realize their full potential: it must provide above all for the best . . . A society which fails to provide adequate support for the next generation of scholars, or for that broad base of skilled and committed researchers who sustain and extend the general pursuit of knowledge and understanding is unlikely to produce many superstars in the future."[3]

The Royal Society reflected elite enthusiasm for the "knowledge economy" and skilfully portrayed universities as the hearts of a sweeping economic transformation. Its message was that Canada's economic prosperity hinged on government support for university research. As a harbinger of debates about "brain drain," the Royal Society cleverly, but without evidence, portrayed university researchers as scarce commodities. Finally, it urged a broad definition of research that embraced humanities and social sciences as well as medicine, engineering, and natural science. The Royal Society's frequent references to social sciences reflected a keen awareness of the ambitions of social scientists to be seen as important within universities, as major researchers and as players in the broader Canadian community.

The Royal Society's strongest message was that society must accommodate itself to the needs of the university not the reverse. Governments were instructed to wake up, to do their duty, and to increase their commitment to universities. The provincial governments, which had not defined university research as a priority, were urged to work with Ottawa. Students were to become more appreciative of faculty research.

The university itself would not change very much. Governments were expected to fund university research. But general and specific research priorities were university business alone. The process of peer review, expert professors assessing the work of other expert professors, was deemed the best process for the selection of research topics and for the judgment of quality. These processes were to remain undisturbed if research was to "realize its potential."

The Royal Society uncritically advanced the mutual enrichment thesis as the foundation of the modern Canadian university. Societal changes, far from undercutting the links between teaching and research, made them even more important. However, the Royal Society saw the research-teaching relationship as one-dimensional. It claimed that research was necessary if teaching was to be relevant and exciting. It made no mention of how research was improved by exposure to undergraduate students. Nor did it prove that research improved teaching. As the report puts it: "Over the years, the educational and research functions of universities have become interdependent and mutually reinforcing. It is now almost universally accepted that all faculty members should be involved in scholarly activity, and that a vigorous research environment is essential to the viability of every university department. Only by being made aware of 'what is happening now' can students come to appreciate the fluidity of knowledge in today's word and to understand the rigorous and complex process by which it is generated."[4]

In all important respects, Stuart Smith's Commission of Inquiry on Canadian University Education differed from the Royal Society. Smith challenged the dominant view that the key problem was government underfunding. In his view, university priorities were also at fault.[5] Smith's ideas profoundly distressed university leadership.

Smith noted the growing importance of published research in Canadian universities. He observed universities' support of specialized faculty research and their emphasis on the quantity of research. Smith also discerned growing professorial preference for research over teaching and a related desire to teach specialized courses. He argued that teaching and research were activities that competed for scarce time and resources. In so doing, he challenged dominant ideas about teaching and research. Smith observed that Canadian universities, despite complaints about government underfunding, were often able to reduce professors' teaching obligations in the face of rising enrolments.

Smith's larger point was that university underfunding was not simply a revenue problem that could be laid at governments' feet. To the contrary, it reflected the very structure of the university itself, which now defined professors as those who taught *and* did research. This core characteristic of universities, especially in an environment where research was dominant and where higher education was widely accessible, meant that professors were teaching less, that research was the priority, and that the university was chronically short of cash. As Smith put it: "The basic idea has been retained that, at a university, the teaching is done by professors who are expected to pursue simultaneously their own scholarly careers. That means that any university system is intrinsically expensive."[6]

Smith was not impressed by university claims about the significance of research. He deflated research when he remarked: "If university professors are being paid to improve their own knowledge and to engage in scholarly activities, it is primarily so that the teaching they offer to successive generations of students will be enriched, and only secondarily because society perceives a need for the research findings themselves."[7] His view was that universities' fundamental obligation is teaching and that research is secondary to teaching. Smith saw higher education as important to society's well-being but made no claims for universities as important forces in the economy.

Ultimately Smith advanced no radical proposals. He conceded that universities should continue to have professors who taught and did research. He also recommended funding increases that would bring Canadian universities more into line with public universities in the United States. He did argue, however, that the teaching obligations should be increased, that all professors should teach every year, and that there should be a floor of teaching commitments.

TEACHING AND RESEARCH: THE MYTH OF MUTUAL ENRICHMENT

Does university research really enhance the quality of teaching and thereby improve students' abilities and life prospects? Are accomplished researchers really better teachers? Is the mutual enrichment thesis an obstacle to serious discussion of university priorities?

Our views are straightforward. We argue that mutual enrichment does not reflect university reality. Teaching and research are generally in conflict with each other. The mutual enrichment thesis is an impediment to necessary university reform. Effective undergraduate teaching, which demands general knowledge, considerable energy, and reflective inquiry, is a very different activity from the preparation of specialized professorial research. Our case rests on three principal sources: scholarly research on the relationship between teaching and research, assessment of university administrative practices, and critical analysis of arguments about mutual enrichment.

University professors have often studied the relationship between teaching and research. Two broad lines of analysis are noteworthy. One strand analyzes student aptitudes and attitudes after exposure to different kinds of universities. A common question is, Do students at research universities have superior abilities as compared with graduates of smaller universities or colleges where teaching is more important than research? Such studies reveal no discernible differences in the performance of students at different kinds of universities. Research universities are not particularly adept at developing students' talents and skills.

A second strand of scholarship probes the relationships between the quality of professors' teaching and research performance. Mutual enrichment ideas imply that excellent researchers should be excellent teachers and weak researchers should fare poorly in the classroom. However, in his exhaustive summary of the studies, Kenneth A. Feldman concludes that, at best, teaching performance is not harmed by research accomplishments. There is no strong positive relation and no strong negative one.[8] Feldman adds that teaching would probably be better if less research was done. The cumulative weight of these findings led Larry Milligan to conclude: "The empirical educational outcomes literature shows that university research intensity does not produce discernible student learning and growth. This is likely due to the simple fact that research and teaching are not, in reality, linked in any meaningful way within our institutions."[9]

The administrative policies of Canadian universities pound spikes into the coffin of mutual enrichment. Universities and government research councils sponsor programs that provide teaching "relief" so that professors can have time to do more research. By their very nature such programs undercut mutual enrichment. They assume that research is accomplished by removing professors from the classroom. In other words, teaching and research are mutually antagonistic. Course buyouts make another point: teaching and research, far from being mutually reinforcing activities, actively compete for professors' time and energy.

A second telling university practice is the extensive use of nonpermanent instructors. Nontenured instructors, who often teach introductory courses, are under no obligation to do research. Many of them are graduate students who are only beginning to know how to do serious research or teach. Only two conclusions are possible in light of this widespread practice. First, either research is not required to be an effective teacher and university practice contradicts university ideology about teaching and research. Or second, if mutual enrichment is true, universities' practice of employing part-time, nonresearching professors is an admission that undergraduates receive an inferior education. Universities cannot logically claim that teaching and research are intertwined to the benefit of students when they employ professors who are not required to do research.

A third dubious administrative practice is the reduction of teaching for new professors so that they can do enough research to gain tenure. If teaching and research interact so that each is improved, why do universities reduce the teaching responsibilities of new professors? The practice arrestingly admits that teaching and research impose contradictory demands on professors. Put differently, young professors who devote their time to undergraduate teaching will be hard pressed to find the time to conduct research. Under these circumstances, it is little wonder that professors, as their careers unfold, come to view effective teaching as an impediment to career advancement. As soon as they enter the university, young professors are encouraged and permitted to trade off teaching for research accomplishments. Professors, seeking tenure, learn behaviours that they never unlearn.[10]

Despite scholarly evidence and their own administrative practices, universities continue to maintain that teaching and research are mutually enriching. Effort is expended on devising elaborate defences of the ideal. Upon examination, university claims about the links between teaching and research are dubious.

Consider the well-known analysis of the relationship between teaching and research by Henry Rosovsky, a former dean of arts and science at Harvard University. Rosovsky pretends to be counselling a talented high school graduate.[11] The issue is whether she should attend a four-year college where the professors emphasize teaching or a research university where professors are "teacher-scholars." In Canada, this is akin to advising a high school student on the relative merits of Mount Allison and the University of Toronto.

Rosovsky's analysis, which strongly implies that such a student should go to a big university, is remarkable in its admissions. The student should go to the research university even though professors are frequently absent, even though a lot of the teaching is done by graduate students, and even though undergraduate students are low priorities for busy research professors.

Rosovsky asserts, without evidence, that university research symbolizes human optimism and a desire to improve society. Accordingly, research professors are optimists. And guess what? Optimists are great teachers! Such comments belie even casual observation of universities whose professors manifest many personality types and mindsets, none of which have ever been linked to performance.

Rosovsky sings the common refrain that research keeps professors intellectually alert and vigorous. Meanwhile, the dedicated teacher becomes deadwood, year after year presenting the same lectures. For Rosovsky, research is the academic profession's antidote to boredom and burnout. As he puts it, "The researcher invests in him- or herself while interacting with an international world of critics and colleagues. These are not activities congenial to deadwood or burned out cases: they cannot share in the stimulation of give and take."[12] Such notions are widely accepted at universities. But they rest on a gross stereotype. Dedicated teachers are burnouts, second-raters, and deadwood. Researchers are dynamic, up-to-date, and exciting. This argument ignores many researchers who are solitary, noncommunicative, and unfriendly to students. It also ignores energetic teachers who are gregarious, who are always at the university arguing with colleagues and supporting their research, and who are deeply admired by students. Second, Rosovsky claims that interaction with other researchers is integral to professorial performance and that professors, who are dedicated to teaching, atrophy when removed from such interaction. But mutual enrichment claims something quite different. It says that professorial research is enriched by teaching, which (obviously) involves interaction with students, not with other professors.

Rosovsky assumes that undergraduate teaching is an inherently tedious task. In a remarkable passage, he notes: "It is hard to see how anyone can teach, say, introductory economics for over a quarter of a century without falling asleep at the very mention of the assignment."[13] On the contrary, how could anyone possibly be bored by such an assignment? The challenges of teaching a complex and important subject could easily sustain an active mind for a lifetime. Can China become genuinely capitalist? Is there really a knowledge economy? How are the mathematical dimensions of modern economics best communicated to beginning students? Does the concept of the household properly value the contribution of women as homemakers? Will there be another Great Depression?

Rosovsky's comments reveal prevailing prejudices toward teaching at universities. The introductory course, despite its innumerable challenges and enormous rewards, is seen as a deadening experience for the professor, who must seek psychological relief and intellectual stimulus from other professors. Rosovsky cultivates an image of professors as busy, influential people whose research and consulting activities are, without argument or evidence, deemed more important than their teaching. Undergraduates are afterthoughts.

The most common assertion about the beneficial links between research and teaching demands a leap of faith. Advocates assert that active researchers, who create knowledge, are by definition better teachers than those who merely transmit knowledge. A related notion is that researchers somehow construct more interesting and relevant courses than others. These views are captured in Jaroslav Pelikan's claim that the most "exciting" teaching is "the communication not of some other scholar's 'existing knowledge' but of one's 'own discovery' in the very process of its being carried on (and revised)."[14] This assertion, music to the ears of modern professors, avoids such hard questions as exciting for whom – professors or students?

What can we say about all this? First, claims about the inherent superiority of researchers as teachers assume that all professorial research is consequential. It implies that university research probes broad, controversial, and significant questions. It also assumes that students need to know about their professors' personal research interests. Second, what does it mean that active researchers advance more interesting and relevant courses? Does anyone who makes this claim examine syllabi? Does anyone ever ask students? Are being up-to-date, exciting, and relevant simply code words for trendy and personally interesting to the professor? More fundamentally, why *in principle* are researchers more interesting, let alone profound, than widely read, thoughtful professors whose focus is students, not other professors? Our analysis of good teaching in Chapter 4 leads us to precisely the opposite conclusion. Finally, claims about the inherent superiority of research professors stress performance in the classroom and formal course content which, while important, are only small parts of effective university teaching. They are silent about the beneficial impact of research on such basic professorial duties as the careful analysis of student work, the development of stimulating assignments, and availability for discussion outside class.[15] Nor do research advocates assert any positive relationships between research excellence and professional conduct, collegiality, and public service.

Teaching and research do reinforce each other in advanced graduate work in natural and medical sciences, where professors and students work together closely on research projects.[16] Here the professor is both teacher and researcher at once. But this model is wrongly imposed in undergraduate studies across the university, where professors are allowed to teach their research. In this way, universities construct a symbiotic relationship between teaching and research where none exists naturally.

Teaching and research also reinforce each other when research is defined as reflective inquiry, which involves disciplined thinking about major questions and wide reading. Reflective inquiry, an obligation of all professors, permits careful examination of the major issues that consume undergraduates. But most professors stress frontier research whose mission is to discover new facts. Such frontier research, contrary to mutual enrichment theory, often harms teaching. The modern professor is highly specialized. He reads narrowly even within his field and is normally far removed from the needs of students for general knowledge and the big picture. Research competes with teaching for professorial time and often involves off-campus travel during term.

TEACHING AND RESEARCH: UNDERLYING POLITICS

We earlier reviewed two different views about the role of Canadian universities. The Royal Society of Canada saw the university as an institution of profound significance. Its professors were often people of national and international reputation. Only a substantial increase in public funding would allow universities to fulfil their crucial mission. On the other hand, the Smith Report saw Canadian universities in more modest terms. He disputed university priorities and argued that teaching must be given higher priority.

The reports differed profoundly about the significance of university research. The Royal Society saw research as essential to economic progress and a robust society. Smith, on the other hand, saw research as subordinate to teaching. The Royal Society endorsed the North American orthodoxy that research and teaching improved each other in modern universities. Smith saw teaching and research as competitive activities.

Canadian professors closed ranks in opposition to the Smith Report. Despite divisions within and between Canadian universities, Smith was a common enemy. For example, even Peter Emberley, a thoughtful critic of universities and an advocate of excellent teaching, dismissed Smith.[17] Emberley felt Smith's report wrongly denigrated research and misunderstood the relationship between teaching and research. Emberley endorsed mutual enrichment when he noted that the classes of nonresearching professors were exercises in "mere information transmission or empty utterance of platitudes."[18] In the same vein, Michiel Horn, in his excellent study of academic freedom, saw Smith's report as an attack on university freedom, particularly in the social sciences and humanities.[19] David Bercuson and his colleagues, who want more research by superstars, mocked Smith.[20] They ridiculed him for not understanding that more teaching will lead to less research!

Why was Smith scorned? Was he not simply advancing well-known American criticisms and endorsing one side of the fractious debate about teaching and research? Such questions are readily answered when one recalls the political functions of mutual enrichment in Canadian universities. The debate, to be understood, must be seen as about the prestige of universities and the social importance of professors.

The idea that teaching and research are mutually enriching confers benefits on the university and its tenured professors. It allows the university to see itself as a unique place where cutting-edge research invigorates teaching. Universities, armed with mutual enrichment ideas, can claim that they are remarkable institutions where teaching and research produce educated citizens *and* economic progress.

Arguments about mutual enrichment embody claims about the unique skills and contributions of professors. Unlike their predecessors who were primarily teachers and thinkers, today's professors can see themselves as doers, exciting people who create knowledge, solve problems, and teach others to do so as well. In their own minds, they are close to the action. Their research allows them to be a role model whose duties are to nurture future researchers and to move students into the knowledge economy armed with a love of research. As recent brain drain debates reveal, the teacher-researcher model can be parlayed into a vision of a sophisticated knowledge worker whose skills are in demand.

Condemnation of the Smith Report reflects universities' desire to protect their status within Canadian society. Advocates of mutual enrichment often imply that today's dominant ideas – that good professors are teachers and frontier researchers – are time honoured. On the contrary, the ideas that university research is vital to society and that professors are multi-skilled persons of consequence are new in Canada. Such ideas were rarely expressed even in the 1960s. Smith's back-to-basics view of universities struck professors as a profound regression that would rob them of their newfound place in the sun. Professors, happy with their emerging status as researchers, their higher salaries, and their reduced classroom obligations, faced the prospect of a forced return to serious undergraduate teaching if Smith's ideas took root. Universities worried about a return to their traditional roles as modest places of basic research and reflective inquiry. The Smith Report made clear to universities that their status was neither universally endorsed nor fully secure.

Universities' opposition to Smith's ideas also reflected their hardening views about their relations with the broader society. The Royal Society's view, that the university was a vital institution that demanded substantial public funding but enjoyed freedom to decide its priorities, was the mainstream. The university was a public body only in the sense that it was primarily funded by taxpayers. In no sense was it an institution whose teaching and research should be shaped by the broader forces of a democratic society. Within the university, each academic discipline was its own master.

It is from this vantage point that one can understand Michiel Horn's argument that Smith's report threatened academic freedom. Implicit in his view is the idea that only universities can decide how to balance their teaching and research. External interventions violated university autonomy. Smith's view, that teaching should assume greater significance, upset universities' relationship with the broader society.

Horn cites Desmond Morton's remark that university research in Canada confronts a "frightening alliance of taxpayers, students and politicians" whose goals are to make teaching more important and to restrict research."[21] This statement, while probably endorsed by many Canadian professors, rests on very questionable grounds. First, no alliance exists of the sort Morton implies. Canadian critics of university research are disparate voices in the wilderness, without formal organization. Second, university research is not under siege by students. Canadian student leaders generally embrace the Royal Society's vision of the university as leader in the knowledge economy and as the site of exciting research. Their agenda is an economic one – lower tuition, better employment prospects, better loan terms – that involves no critical analysis of university priorities. Third, several provincial governments – Manitoba, Quebec, Ontario, and Alberta are examples – have occasionally complained about excessive university research. None has ever gone beyond casual sabre-rattling. The federal government, for its part, has parlayed support for university research and university students into a pillar of its programs for Canada in the twenty-first century. Even a casual observer of public affairs can easily detect unwavering support for university research in the policies of the Chrétien Liberals, especially since 1995.

Canadian universities are united on such basic matters as the importance of research, university control over research priorities, and mutual enrichment. A natural force of dissent, and an obvious advocate of superior teaching, is the Faculties of Arts, which comprise humanities like English, social sciences like economics, and fine arts like music. As we have noted, professors in arts, driven by a desire to be as respected as scientists, are now true believers in research and mutual enrichment. They see research, not teaching or reflective inquiry, as their passports to university status and influence in society.

CONCLUSION

Canadian universities portray themselves as unique institutions where teaching and research dovetail for the well-being of students and society. Unfortunately, university reform will be difficult until the idea that teaching and research enrich each other is banished. The idea will not fade easily because it confirms status on professors and importance on universities.

Rigid adherence to mutual enrichment blinds universities to an obvious point – superb teaching can be done without reference to research and outstanding research can be done without exposure to teaching. Meaningful debate about what universities should do, about how they should relate to other research institutions, and about what should be taught are impeded by mutual enrichment. To make matters worse, all universities believe in mutual enrichment. Smaller universities now want their professors to do research. They resist debate about whether they should downplay research and stress teaching. Small universities do not want to be seen as mere teaching colleges.

Within universities, the idea that some faculties should teach more (Faculties of Arts and Science are obvious examples) are resisted in principle. Mutual enrichment asserts that professors, to be effective, must be cutting-edge researchers. The idea that English professors, for example, should have a heavier teaching load than professors of chemical engineering is seen as heresy. Mutual enrichment dogma also impedes meaningful reform of academic careers. From time to time, universities have argued that professors should be encouraged to choose teaching or research streams in their careers. A variation is the idea that professors should be able to emphasize one area or the other at different points. Such ideas invariably flounder under the weight of mutual enrichment. Professors who aren't absorbed in frontier research are seen as second class, lazy, and ineffective. The debate is over before it begins.

In the United States, controversy about teaching and research is more heated than in Canada. One line of attack is to define away the problem by arguing that learning is the issue, not the interaction between teaching and research.[22] This effort has failed. As Donald Kennedy puts it, "It is clear that a single issue, division of labor between teaching and research, is affecting the quality of life for many in the professoriate."[23]

A second American response is to resolve tensions between teaching and research by tilting university programs toward research, by exposing even first-year students to research, and by constructing links between faculty research and teaching as a matter of university policy. This view achieved prominence after the release of the Boyer Commission's report entitled *Reinventing Undergraduate Education: A Blueprint for America's Research Universities.* The late Ernest Boyer, a well-known observer of higher education, and a commission of distinguished Americans condemned large American universities for their neglect of undergraduate students. Boyer lauded American research universities as institutions of great accomplishment. But his commission pulled no punches when it noted the heavy emphasis on faculty publication, the excessive use of graduate students as undergraduate instructors, and the uninspired approach to undergraduate teaching on America's major campuses.

We agree with Boyer's concerns about the inferior quality of undergraduate teaching. We also worry about his solution. He argued that teaching and research are potentially compatible but that university practices would have to change if mutual enrichment was to be a day-to-day reality. In other words, teaching and research did not naturally reinforce one but they could be made to do so. Boyer wanted all students to understand research, to see researchers in practice, and to engage in research from the start to the finish of their university careers. Professors would be encouraged to expose undergraduates to specialized research and to integrate their research into class work. Boyer wanted to make faculty research, undergraduate education, and graduate studies a seamless web.

Boyer's ideas merit serious consideration. But is his plan feasible? First, undergraduate students might well be excited by exposure to first-class research. But can they really grasp advanced research when they know no fundamentals? Second, undergraduates need and want systematic exposure to the great issues of human society. Efforts to fuse teaching and research may work against general education. Professors will want to convert courses into seminars on their own work. As a result, the curriculum will be even more driven by professorial preferences not students' needs. Third, we think that effective undergraduate teaching is an activity that should be kept separate from professors' frontier research. Undergraduates need a curriculum that is broad and deep, professors who devote full energy to their needs, and courses based on thoughtful analysis of their educational needs.

CHAPTER 7

ETHICS IN CANADIAN UNIVERSITIES

On 24 August 1992, Valery Fabrikant, a research professor in the Faculty of Engineering and Computer Science at Concordia University in Montreal, shot and killed four of his male colleagues and seriously wounded a female secretary. No one has, or could, make a case that these were justifiable homicides. It is most unlikely that Fabrikant had anything in particular against the four colleagues he murdered. And probably the secretary just happened to be at the wrong place at the wrong time. The wrong place was Concordia's Henry F. Hall building. The wrong time was when Professor Fabrikant finally snapped and lashed out in rage against those he believed were his oppressors, exploiters, and tormentors. Unfortunately, he had reason to believe that he was a victim of exploitation. A brief examination of his career at Concordia – what was done to him, what he did to others, and especially the various reactions to his conduct – illuminates several serious ethical issues in Canadian universities.

On 18 December 1979, Fabrikant, still a Soviet citizen but holding a US green card, arrived at the office of T.S. Sankar, chair of the Department of Mechanical Engineering at Concordia University, looking for a job. Sankar did not make it a practice to see people without an appointment, so the secretary turned him away. Still without an appointment, however, Fabrikant got to see Sankar the next day. Apparently Sankar was impressed. He appointed Fabrikant as his research assistant, a position that requires the skills of a high-level technician. This was the first day of Fabrikant's almost thirteen years of employment at Concordia. During this period he caused many people huge amounts of stress and distress.[1]

T.S. Sankar granted Fabrikant several sizable raises in salary, some part-time teaching, and a promotion. In 1980, Fabrikant began to coauthor scholarly articles with Sankar. In 1982, Sankar recommended to the dean of the Faculty of Engineering and Computer Science, Dr. M.N.S. Swamy, that Fabrikant be appointed to the most junior academic faculty position, that of research assistant professor. The position was offered and accepted. This change of salary and status was simply a recognition that Fabrikant was not really working as a supervised technician. He was working quite inde-pendently as an applied mathematician and deserved faculty status. Never-theless, none of Fabrikant's major job changes at Concordia was filled according to standard university practice, which requires the announce-ment of a vacancy so that others may compete for it. In the same year, 1982, Dean Swamy joined Sankar as coauthor with Fabrikant of journal articles.

In 1983, Fabrikant became embroiled in one of the several nasty incidents for which he became notorious. In that year he took a French-language course in Concordia's Continuing Education program. As a special favour to Fabrikant, fees for the course were waived. Before long, Fabrikant began making extremely insulting remarks about the teacher's methods and accent. Soon he became so abusive that both the teacher and other students threatened to quit the course. Two Continuing Education officials barred Fabrikant from the course. He responded by attending the next class and tearing up the letter of expulsion in front of the teacher and students. Finally, the director of Continuing Education barred Fabrikant from all Continuing Education classes, and he obeyed that order.

In 1985, after another promotion and several increases in salary, Fabrikant was transferred to the Concordia Computer Aided Vehicle Engineering Centre (CONCAVE), a new organization connected to the Concordia en-gineering faculty and funded by the Government of Quebec. The director of CONCAVE was Dr. Seshadri Sankar, brother of T.S. Sankar, Fabrikant's former supervisor. For a few years, Fabrikant was more or less tolerable, but in 1989 he returned to form.

The provocation for Fabrikant's new round of disruption seems to have been the denial of his application for early promotion. To say that this development upset Fabrikant would be a huge understatement. He claimed that others were getting unfair advantage from his research and that some of his colleagues engaged in "questionable publishing." Moreover, he started to make veiled threats of violence, including a vow to "get" the rector (the person known as president at most universities). Nevertheless, Fabrikant was appointed to a tenure-track position as associate professor in 1990. Things quieted down for a while.

Soon, however, Fabrikant was at it again, both zanier and more threatening than ever. He began to quarrel openly with colleagues, especially Dr. T.S. Sankar's successor as chair of the mechanical engineering department. At first this took the form of nasty personal letters to people at Concordia. Before long, though, he began to expand the letter campaign and then switched to electronic mail. Soon he was circulating by e-mail throughout North America allegations about the academic and scientific integrity of several of his colleagues. His principal targets were Tom Sankar, his brother Seshadri Sankar, and M.N.S. Swamy.[2] Many of Fabrikant's accusations were preposterous. An example is his claim that T.S. Sankar had made no scientific contribution, at any time in his career, to any of the numerous articles that listed him as author or coauthor. But some of his accusations were well founded. For example, S. Sankar obtained a contract for a company he owned when he should have sought it for CONCAVE, the Concordia research centre of which he was the director and which was set up to do precisely the kind of work specified in the contract.

Fabrikant was right, above all, about some of his colleagues' lack of decent standards for claiming coauthorship of scientific publications. He proved this point himself by working sting operations against Professors T. Sankar and Swamy. The background to the sting was Fabrikant's publication in 1971, in a Russian academic periodical, of an important article in applied mathematics. Beginning in 1981, he began to "recycle" this article with various coauthors, starting with T.S. Sankar. With only slight modifications, versions of this paper were published in academic journals in the United States, Germany, France, and Great Britain. The sting was that Dr. Sankar and later Dr. Swamy allowed (or perhaps encouraged) Fabrikant to list them as coauthors of the articles, even though they could not have made a substantial contribution to any of them.

Although Fabrikant made numerous requests to various appropriate bodies, both inside and outside the university, to have his charges investigated, no one carried out a searching investigation – before the murders.

By the spring of 1992, Fabrikant had intensified his e-mail campaign and threats of lawsuits to the point of obsession. On 22 June, he applied for employer endorsement for a handgun transport permit. This application caused real alarm, particularly in view of the fact that it implied that Fabrikant already possessed at least one handgun. The application worked its way up the university hierarchy and was rejected by the rector on 14 July. The rector did not use his emergency powers to suspend Fabrikant and no legal measures were taken to bar him from the Concordia campus. Probably unbeknownst to Fabrikant, steps were being taken that could have led to his dismissal, and there was movement toward commissioning an external inquiry into his complaints about research ethics. But all this was rendered moot by the massacre of 24 July.

We want to stress bluntly that situations as extreme as the Fabrikant case are not regular occurrences on Canadian campuses. Nevertheless, this situation illustrates in dramatic form common ethical problems at Canadian universities. Indeed, the sorry tale of Fabrikant at Concordia touches on most of the moral issues facing contemporary Canadian universities: conflict of interest, neglect of duty, abuse of authority as well as failure to exercise authority courageously and effectively, inattention to undergraduate students, and, in general, lackadaisical teaching, profoundly nasty and disruptive conduct toward colleagues; harassment, and academic dishonesty so persistent and profound that it deserves the label "academic corruption." Again, it should go without saying that extreme threats of violence and murder are rare on Canadian campuses. We do not deal here with conduct that is monstrously evil or unjust, not just because it is rare but also because "monstrously evil or unjust" does not call for elaboration. Nor will we deal with an array of minor vices that are not central to the main ethical issues confronted by universities.

We begin by examining critically the main responses to the Fabrikant affair. We discuss these responses by relating them to the old saw about a few bad apples spoiling the whole barrel. The simplest view is that there was only one bad apple, Fabrikant himself. He was either insane, or evil, or both, and that's the whole story. Some press accounts hint at this explanation but it was not given much credence. This view does have the merit that it affirms that the actions of an individual are the responsibility of that individual not the intersection of a set of social forces. If Fabrikant hadn't chosen to shoot people, he wouldn't have killed them. Beyond that, the bad apple view casts little light on the Fabrikant affair.

More illuminating views are presented in the three external inquiries commissioned by Concordia's board of governors. The first, published in April 1994, was entitled *Integrity in Scholarship: A Report to Concordia University*. It is more commonly known as the Arthurs Report, after the chair of the three-person committee that prepared it, Harry Arthurs, a law professor and former president of York University. The second, published in May 1994, was entitled *Lessons from the Fabrikant File*. It was prepared by John Scott Cowan, an Ottawa consultant in the training of academic administrators. The third was a study conducted by a forensic accountant of Concordia's accounting procedures and the financial manipulations of some of Fabrikant's colleagues.[3]

A more plausible view of the bad apple view is that there were several bad apples. Fabrikant, of course, was one, but so were several entrepreneurs in his faculty, who spent hugely excessive amounts of time consulting and employing their research skills in their own companies or those of their associates, while wrongly acquiring coauthorship of papers produced by colleagues and graduate students. Other bad apples were various university officials, from department chairs to the chief financial officers to the rector, and possibly even the university ombudsperson. They were guilty mainly of sins of omission (failure to exercise their authority effectively and decisively) rather than commission. Suggestions of this kind are subthemes in all three of the reports under consideration. The many bad apples view is certainly more plausible than the one bad apple view. However, the several bad apples view suffers from the same limitation as the single bad apple view. Although it says, correctly, that when we behave badly we are perpetrators, not victims, it doesn't tell us why we have bad apples or how we can prevent the rot from spreading.

An alternative view is that the problem was not – or at least not mainly – with the apples but with the barrel itself. This is the view of John Scott Cowan, who was a consultant on university management and is now principal of the Royal Military College of Canada. Not surprisingly, Cowan thinks that university officials are the barrel that shapes the relationships among the apples. If the barrel is not sound in construction, apples are sure to rot, and the rot is sure to spread rapidly. Cowan's central position is that academic administrators have to be well trained and tough. He states this view in the following passage:

> At no time after 1989 (when concern had begun to mount) did any senior officer of the institution confront Dr. Fabrikant in the personal and almost brutal drawing of the line which occasionally works with persons whose disorders are those attributed by the University's consultants to Dr. Fabrikant. Nor, without particular training and practical experience, would I have expected them to feel able to do so. Nonetheless, there have been numerous instances in Canadian universities, of a senior officer calling in a faculty member and saying (more or less), "Dear Professor X, in the conversation which follows, I want you to understand that for all practical purposes, I am your employer. I do not like what you are doing. I will now give you chapter and verse about what I do not like ... (does exactly that) ... I am now instructing you, as your employer, never to do any similar thing again, or I will fire you. This is a legal instruction. I will confirm it in writing. If you ever have any doubt about whether you are about to do something which may breach this legal instruction, call me and ask me, bearing in mind that the content, conduct and context of that call might also breach this instruction. Now get out."[4]

Cowan's view that academic administrators would profit from training in how to deal with exceptionally disruptive or threatening people (be they other administrators, professors, or students) is indisputable. Nevertheless, we find his proposals generally unhelpful and in some major respects wrong. First, we think Cowan's assessment of the typical career paths of academic administrators is misleading. His view is stated early in his report: "One must understand," he says, "that the majority of academic administrators do not like administration itself, do not think of themselves as administrators, have no training for their administrative roles other than popular television shows and modest on the job exposure, and are accustomed to work in a milieu where the exercise of authority is considered in bad taste ... Giving an order, even a reasonable one, is anathema to many."[5]

Contrary to Cowan's view, people who become chairs of academic departments do so mainly because they want to become administrators. Certainly they don't do it for the money. Administrative stipends at this level don't compensate for the headaches. Moreover, during the severe financial restraint of the 1990s, a chair had few opportunities to put her mark on a department by creative hiring. With rare exceptions, only people who have served as department chairs become deans. The next level, vice-president, consists exclusively of people who have had a good deal of previous experience in academic administration.[6] Behind vice-presidents are additional ambitious administrators, associate and assistant vice-presidents, all with plenty of experience in administration, waiting to move up, either at their present university or another. Typically, university presidents start climbing the ladder young, move through all the stages – chair, dean, vice-president – and leave themselves enough time to move from the presidency of one university to that of a bigger and more prestigious one. Universities are not filled with professors who became deans, much less vice-presidents, only to return happily to teaching and research. University presidents seldom return to the professors' daily grind. Cowan's vision of university administrators as babes in the woods is just wrong. Often at the level of department chair, and invariably at the level of president, senior university administrators are experienced, hard-nosed executives. It is true that they don't run around giving orders to professors. But that is proof of prudence not timidity.

Second, Cowan's assessment ignores the power of university professors. Canadian universities have certainly become more bureaucratized in the last three decades. They are not now (and never were) run as democratic "communities of scholars." Still, professors have a long tradition of considerable independence, a shorter but well-established tradition of professionalism and legal guarantees of academic freedom. They also have academic staff associations or unions to protect their interests. Any administrator unwise enough to treat a professor as Cowan recommends – that is, in the manner of the owner of a small family business – would not only fail to achieve his objectives but also would find himself in deep trouble. The very suggestion that a university administrator could treat a professor as an employee and threaten to fire him because he doesn't "like" what the professor does is ludicrous. To return to our apples and barrel analogy, it is a mistake to think that the barrel is composed of administrators. The barrel is formed in large part by the professors themselves. So if the barrel needs fixing, the professors need fixing, and administrators are in no position to do all or even most of the repairs.

The most impressive of the three reports, the Arthurs Report, maintains that the central problem is neither with the apples nor with the barrel but with the market in which barrels of apples are produced and exchanged. Arthurs begins with a diagnosis of the situation at Concordia, particularly in the Faculty of Engineering and Computer Science: "In some quarters, ever-higher activity levels, ever-growing output, bigger and better grants and contracts, more and more equipment and facilities, higher and higher graduate enrolments, have become ends in themselves. Worse yet, they have become ends which are sometimes used to justify means which are highly questionable."[7]

A great merit of the Arthurs Report is the breadth of its interests. It does not confine its attention to a single faculty at Concordia or even to Concordia as a whole. Indeed, its authors note that the serious problems they identify are not unique to Concordia: "They have their origins not in the intrinsic wickedness of any of the persons involved nor in particular defects of [Concordia's] administrative structures. Rather, they are the almost inescapable pathology of the surrounding research culture, of systems of scholarly assessment, research funding and industry-university-government cooperation which have developed in Canada over the past 25 years, and ultimately of developments in scholarship which, if not universal, are certainly widespread."[8]

What, then, is the root of the problem, according to the Arthurs Report? It is that "research, especially in the physical sciences and engineering [and, we should add, the medical sciences], has become both highly specialized and very expensive." Such research requires considerable funding, which, under the current rules of the game, "depends upon a demonstrated capacity to 'produce' results." However, production "can come to be measured primarily in terms of the quantity of units of output, rather than their quality, and to be maximized for its own sake, without regard to the externalities – the social, economic, cultural and environmental consequences – which it generates." The result is that "too often university honours, research grants and industrial contracts are awarded on the basis of numbers of publications, rather than on their quality and significance."

The principal conclusion reached in the Arthurs Report is that "the issue of production-driven research is a challenge not just for Concordia, but for the entire Canadian Research community." Furthermore, this is not a challenge that can be met simply by asserting noble principles or setting out rules of conduct. According to Arthurs and his colleagues, "Nothing less than a change in the culture and context of research will suffice. Public and private sector providers of research funds must reexamine the underlying assumptions and visible consequences of their funding strategies. Collegial and administrative committees concerned with resource allocation, hiring, promotion, tenure, merit pay, and honours must revisit the premises upon which they assess and reward scholarly accomplishment. Academic unions must reconsider their willingness to defend professorial autonomy when it is used not to advance academic freedom but rather for self-aggrandizement."[9]

This is the central point. Probably bad apples are not more numerous in universities than elsewhere, nor barrels more weakly constructed. However, there are serious and worsening problems in the apple market. Therefore, if we are to improve the quality of the apples, we have to improve the market. Put directly, unethical conduct that originates in universities is probably neither more frequent nor more serious than in other walks of life. There is no good reason to believe that university students, professors, and administrators are, as individuals, more inclined to lie, cheat, harass, defraud, or bully than steelworkers, nurses, or journalists. Furthermore, even if university campuses were populated by people morally inferior to the rest of the population, there would be little that could be done about that in the short run. Improving the moral character of administrators, staff, and students would be the work of at least a generation. There are only two ways to improve the moral quality of universities in the short term. First, we can strengthen the incentives to behave well. Second, we can eliminate, or at least reduce, the incentives to behave badly. Neither of these alternatives should be ignored. In light of these alternatives, we now take up the main ethical issues confronting universities.

CONFLICT OF INTEREST

In recent years the term "conflict of interest" has been used very loosely. We use it quite strictly to refer to a situation in which a person benefits materially himself, his family, his friends, or his associates by violating his occupational duties. (Thus, the conflict is between his material interests and his occupational interests.) A familiar example of conflict of interest is that of the city councillor who owns real estate that could appreciate in value depending on the vote on a zoning bylaw. As a matter of ethics, and almost always as a matter of law as well, the councillor is prohibited from voting on the bylaw in question. Upright councillors refrain from voting whenever it would result in a conflict of interest.

Conflicts of interest in universities arise when professors have commercial interests that conflict with their professional duties to engage in teaching, research, and public service. There were conflicts of interest connected with the Fabrikant case. Such conflicts were aggravated, if not created, by government policies that gave preference in the awarding of research grants to private companies over universities. These policies encouraged senior members of the Faculty of Engineering and Computer Science at Concordia to set up private companies to acquire grants instead of acquiring grants for the faculty. Some of them apparently required little encouragement. They set up private companies and profited by doing research in their capacity as businesspeople rather than professors. There were conflicts of interest that were motivated both by the lack of scruples of the people involved in them and by public policies. In other words, they were motivated both by the presence of bad apples and by the character of the apple market.

Even in the Concordia faculty, with its lax academic standards and high tolerance of commercial science, conflicts of interest were not the main problem. Fabrikant was affected by others' conflicts of interest, but they did not play a major role in his case. There is no reason to believe that the situation is worse at other Canadian universities. There are conflicts of interest, but they are probably few and relatively small in importance.

NEGLECT OF DUTY

Neglect of duty was endemic in the Fabrikant case. Fabrikant's associates in the Faculty of Engineering and Computer Science concentrated their energies so closely on production of publications and on the acquisition of grants and contracts to facilitate still more publications that they had little time for other professorial duties. A senior member of the faculty attempted to explain a rate of publication of academic papers that seems humanly impossible on grounds that would be amusing if they were not so shocking. First, he said that he had taught no students for over a decade. Second, he interpreted the university regulation that allowed professors to work as consultants only one day a week as permitting consulting and research work for his private business every evening and every weekend. In other words, he acknowledged, apparently without shame, that he did nothing that was recognizably academic except for a bit of administration. He taught no students, engaged in no dialogue with his colleagues, and performed no public service related to his professional competence. He did nothing but engage in specialized consulting and research. In short, he ignored most of his professorial duties.

The neglect of duty that was commonplace in Concordia's engineering faculty was undoubtedly unusual in its extent and its brazenness. However, the same factors that reached pathological dimensions at Concordia are at work in other universities. We should recall the reference in the Arthurs Report, quoted earlier in this chapter, to "the almost inescapable pathology of the surrounding research culture, of systems of scholarly assessment, research funding and industry-university-government cooperation which have developed in Canada over the past 25 years, and ultimately of developments in scholarship which, if not universal, are certainly widespread."

When we asked scientists at several Canadian universities if something quite similar to the Fabrikant case could happen at their university, almost everyone gave us the same answer: a qualified "yes." The "yes" was qualified everywhere for the same reason: that single-minded concentration on research, especially on commercially applicable research, had not gone so far elsewhere as at Concordia. However, almost all our respondents acknowledged that strong pressures to publish voluminously were a powerful incentive to neglect other professorial duties. Moreover, there was a general recognition that the pressures to publish profusely originate outside any particular university. With rare exceptions, professors secure recognition outside their own university only for their publications. University departments, in turn, are judged by their "productive scholars." And universities are judged by their departments. Thus, professors and university officials have an incentive to emphasize research and downplay other professorial duties. Once again, the problem is not bad apples but the badness of the apple market.

ABUSE OF AUTHORITY

Authority was abused in two quite different ways during the Fabrikant debacle. Some people in positions of authority used that authority vigorously for thoroughly illegitimate purposes. Others failed to exercise their authority when they should have.

As Fabrikant's sting proved, his immediate superiors were quite prepared to share credit for the intellectual work of subordinates to which they did not make any contribution. There is actually a double immorality here. First, there is intellectual dishonesty. It is simply wrong to take credit for the work of others. An essay written by my associate is not partly my essay simply because I stimulated him to think about his topic in a more fruitful way. Nor does it become partly my essay because I read it critically and suggested helpful improvements, although at this point some acknowledgement of assistance is probably due. I am coauthor of an essay only if I made a significant contribution to its composition.

The second immorality is exploitation by superiors of inferiors in a structure of authority. Fabrikant saw that he could promote security and advancement in his job if he gave his bosses credit for work they did not do. Exploitation is not always, or even typically, a matter of explicit bribes and threats. Unspoken understandings that illegitimate services will be rewarded are both more typical and more difficult to resist.

There is a problem in parts of some scientific and technological disciplines that smacks of both intellectual dishonesty and abuse of authority. In some scientific subdisciplines the research unit is a team that is headed by a senior professor. The team leader manages the laboratory in which the team members work: it is "her lab." The team leader determines the projects on which the team works. It is she who gets the grants necessary to maintain the lab and the team. A long-standing practice is that publications emanating from a lab are deemed to be the work of most, if not all, team members, so they are listed as coauthors whether or not they made any substantial contribution to the publication. In particular, the team leader is invariably listed as a coauthor. Indeed, she is sometimes named first in a list of coauthors, even if she made no identifiable contribution to the publication.

It is tempting to censure unequivocally the practice described in the preceding paragraph as involving both intellectual dishonesty and abuse of authority. To condemn too quickly and too vociferously would be a mistake because the practice has become so deeply embedded that no individual and no single university could put an end to it. The survival of a team depends on the production of a steady flow of research publications. If the team leader is not listed as coauthor of enough publications, grant money dries up. Without grants there is no lab and no team. Again, the problem is the apple market, not the individual apples.

Nevertheless, it is dishonest to take credit for the work of others. But here we may be seeing the first steps toward a story with a happy ending. Some scientific associations and scientific periodicals have confronted the problem and are taking steps to devise procedures for ensuring that credit is given only where it is due. This is an encouraging recognition that the remedy for some moral abuses is reform of a system of relationships rather than the repentance of individual sinners.

Abuse of authority during the Fabrikant affair was a matter not only of exercising authority illegitimately but also of failure to exercise it when there was a crying need to do so. There were numerous instances of this shortcoming but the most consequential were the inactions subsequent to Fabrikant's implicit and explicit threats of violence. Above all, no one in a senior administrative post took the obvious first step of calling the police and bringing them prominently into the picture. It is tempting to accuse the senior administrators of moral cowardice and to find the solution to the problem in recruitment of administrators with more backbone. The amount of unseemly buck-passing attempted by senior Concordia administrators strengthens this temptation. However, once again we must consider the apple market and not just individual apples.

Senior university administrators in Canada are essentially men and women whose main tasks are to raise funds, recruit students, and hold down costs while maintaining good relations with governments and the professors. These qualities are not strongly correlated with decisive action in emergencies.

INSUFFERABLE CONDUCT

Fabrikant should have been severely reprimanded long before he was, and, failing timely reprimands, he should have been suspended and enjoined from entering the Concordia campus during his suspension. In a university, obnoxious conduct can be more than a vice. Beyond certain limits, it should be grounds for withholding rewards, imposing sanctions, suspension, and (in the worst cases) dismissal.

That said, universities should be very cautious in judging conduct as insufferable for two main reasons. First, a propensity to censure can lead to injustices to individuals. Canadians generally, and Canadian university professors particularly, tend to judge timid and brash people very differently. We tend to be very tolerant of the vices of the timid. Instead of taking them to task for their frequent failure to stand up and be counted, we tend to pity their shyness, their vulnerability to harsh words, and their fear of confrontation. In contrast, we tend to exaggerate the vices of the brash. Instead of praising them for their intrepidity, we often see the confident, the opinionated, and the outspoken as brazen, overbearing, and arrogant. Therefore, incautiousness about judging conduct as insufferable may victimize the brash.

The second reason why we should be cautious about labelling the conduct of professors or students as insufferable is that universities flourish when unconventional views, theories, methodologies, and styles of expression are not merely tolerated but actively encouraged. Universities work best when debate centres on people's ideas rather than their personalities. The last thing universities need is a spirit of censoriousness.

To say that in universities we should be cautious about judging conduct as insufferable is not to say that we should never do so. Some conduct *is* insufferable.

When we think about which instances of insufferable conduct in universities should be penalized, we see pretty quickly that the position of those who are more tolerant of timidity than brashness, though morally weak, has the virtue (so to speak) of realism. Keeping silent in the face of large evils is no doubt worse than committing small ones. Nevertheless, attempting to punish spinelessness would be a case of the cure being worse than the disease. We mention only three problems. What would count as evidence that someone was guilty of insufferable timidity? (How could anyone counter her claim that she didn't know about the problem, or how bad it was?) What manageable steps could be taken to ensure charges of spinelessness were not made randomly? (How could anyone counter her claim that she was being used as a scapegoat – that the timidity of many others had been ignored?) How could excuses be handled? (How could anyone counter her claim that she didn't blow the whistle because she was afraid that the old boys would brand her as a whiner?) Even though doing nothing is, in a moral sense, doing something (namely, refraining from doing the right thing), the practical obstacles to punishing silence are insuperable.

Which types of conduct are insufferable? We need not pause over insufferable conduct that is also illegal. Murder, assault, threats of bodily harm, defamation, and so on are not problematical. Harassment of all types should fall into the same category.

There are two problem areas regarding insufferable conduct. The first is comportment that goes beyond brashness to the point where it is better described as overbearing, imperious, or even bullying. The problem is that it is very difficult to determine when the line has been crossed between the former and the latter. Of course no definitive answer emerges. We confine ourselves to suggesting two considerations that help distinguish between what is merely offensive and what is genuinely harmful. The first is whether or not the offending behaviour exhibits a persistent pattern of inhibiting the expression of opposing opinions. Universities thrive on freedom of speech; persistently inhibiting it is insufferable. The second consideration is that the tenderest souls among the professoriate should not be given undue weight in drawing the line. Universities attract a sizable minority of people who are intimidated by the very prospect that their views may be contested vigorously. Since universities depend on dialogue, the scope and style of permissible dialogue should not be decided by those who are least respectful of vigorous debate.

The second major problem has to do with exploitation. There is, to our knowledge, no disagreement with the proposition that exploitation (the extraction of favours through the illegitimate exercise of power or threat to exercise power) is insufferable conduct. The problem is that all but the most casual relationships between people involve at least some element of power. Accordingly, the issue is not between relationships that involve power and those that do not but between those in which power is more or less reciprocal and those in which there is such an imbalance of power that exploitation is almost unavoidable. Once again we face an issue that has no definitive answer. We have only one recommendation to assist in drawing the line. Universities should avoid paternalism as far as possible. We illustrate this generalization with reference to rules regarding sexual relationships between professors and students. The extremes are no rules at all (which is blanket permission) and blanket prohibition. Blanket permission is fraught with unavoidable bad consequences. Obviously, professors should not become involved sexually with students they are currently teaching. It is hardly less evident that they should not become involved with students whose university careers they are in a position to affect significantly. Some American universities have gone to the extreme of blanket prohibition. This policy treats students as though they have learned nothing from their lifelong encounters with power. It is insufferably paternalistic.

In summary, not only in extreme cases like that of Fabrikant but also in the less dramatic day-to-day life of universities, there are instances of insufferable behaviour. They should be grounds for withholding rewards, imposing sanctions, suspension, and (in the worst cases) dismissal. However, universities should be extremely cautious about judging conduct as insufferable. In particular, it is important to avoid victimizing the brash, setting standards of civility designed to coddle tender souls, or extending paternalism beyond the narrowest possible scope.

CONCLUSION

In extreme form, the Fabrikant case exhibited many ethical problems faced by contemporary universities, including conflict of interest, neglect of duty, and abuse of authority as well as failure to exercise authority effectively and nasty behaviour toward colleagues. Such a range of issues demands careful reconsideration of the moral obligations of professors and universities.

On these points, we reached two main conclusions. First, personal moral responsibility is inescapable. People are responsible for their choices and for the conduct motivated by their choices. This is true generally, but it is particularly pertinent to what we call insufferable conduct. Our second conclusion, which is less commonplace and more germane to efforts at reform, is that most of the leading moral abuses in Canadian universities are best understood relationally. We made much of the old saying about the bad apple that spoils the whole barrel. We found that most ethical problems in Canadian universities stem not from bad apples or even bad barrels but from characteristics of the apple market. More plainly, major ethical problems stem from pressures to publish voluminously, which bring scholars and universities into a competition for the wherewithal – prestige, personnel, grants, and contracts – that makes prolific publication possible.

CHAPTER 8

UNIVERSITIES IN BUSINESS

Issues and Prospects

In the early twenty-first century, Canadian universities are debating the commercialization of scholarly life. The debate is complex and straightforward at the same time. At its heart is the claim that universities are major forces in the economy.

We have already noted that Canadian universities have been closely linked to the national economy, especially since the end of the Second World War.[1] They are Canada's primary source of skilled scientific and medical personnel. University research, both basic and applied, in science, engineering, and medicine is a recognized determinant of Canada's economic prowess.

The commercial university adds controversial new dimensions, since some universities now see themselves as producers of commercially viable products and processes, as agents of national economic policies, and as partners of businesses. The results of university research are sometimes seen as revenue sources for universities. Such ideas have replaced worries that universities are ivory towers with fears that they are too close to business.

In the early twenty-first century, universities emphasize science, technology, and student employability. Critics claim that universities have been seduced by the modern world's admiration of business.[2] Using overstatement, one critic notes that North American universities want to attract money, study money, and make money.[3]

The trend toward more applied research raises questions about university objectivity and about the capacity of universities to analyze society. It also evokes concerns about power within the university, about conflicts of interest as faculty mesh business and scholarly roles, and about the further deterioration of teaching as a university priority.

We doubt that commercial pressures will dominate Canadian universities. Those who gloomily predict the transformation of universities into technology factories underestimate the commitment of many academic scientists to basic research and conventional scholarly publication. Moreover, commercial science is a quite understandable development in research universities. It grows in environments that downplay teaching, that stress research in the first instance, and that need large amounts of research funding. Critics sometimes fiercely attack commercial science as though it were a radical departure from an ideal status quo.

This chapter has three parts. First, it deals with several commercial characteristics of Canadian universities. These include fundraising, advertising, and the use of modern management practices. The chapter then examines the most controversial aspect of commercialization: close links between universities and companies in the conduct of scientific research. We use the term "commercial science" to describe this trend. Finally, the chapter examines the future of the commercial university. We see commercial forces as worrisome but not as dominant or irreversible.

Readers will find the tone and judgments of this chapter much more guarded than elsewhere in the book. This is so because commercial science raises issues and problems whose full consequences are unclear to us. University phenomena such as fundraising and applied research are not inherently corrupting of university ideals. Like "pure" research and teaching, they can be done in ways that debase universities or in ways that strengthen universities. No iron laws present themselves.

Three tests are applied to evaluate commercial activities of universities. First, does the activity distort university priorities? Second, does the activity prevent the university from retaining or changing its priorities? Third, does the activity undermine collegiality and established decision-making processes? Such criteria are more readily stated than applied. In practice, it is often difficult to determine the full impact of commercial activities. Complex evidence must be weighed that demands careful judgment.

SOFT COMMERCIALIZATION

Fundraising

Canadian universities have long undertaken fundraising aimed principally at alumni. Early in the new millennium, universities have professional fundraisers usually led by a vice-president of "external relations," "development" or "advancement." Such officials often have extensive contacts beyond campus. They come from many walks of life, but few are professors or have been professors. Fundraisers' principal undertaking is capital campaigns that try to raise multimillion-dollar amounts. In this endeavour, corporations and wealthy individuals are the targets.

Fundraising tries to diversify university revenues and to thereby avoid excessive dependence on governments. In this sense, fundraising tries to increase universities' independence of action. It is shaped by long-standing, often very successful, efforts by American universities to solicit corporate and alumni support.

Fundraising at Canadian universities gives power to administrators and fundraisers who may have limited understanding of, and commitment to, university ideals. The goals of campaigns, the detailed on-campus distribution of funds raised, and the process of fundraising itself are seldom debated through established university channels.

Fundraising may also distort university priorities, although such distortion is not automatic. Distortion occurs because donors give for specific reasons and in support of specific purposes. In this regard, Canadian universities can claim neither innocence nor ignorance. For decades American university presidents have acknowledged that large donors want something in return.[4] Moreover, universities sometimes take donations even when it causes them to move in new directions and even when it causes them to spend money to support new donor-sponsored activities. The problem is serious when universities receive money for new buildings and major equipment. Such physical plants must be maintained and operated – donations seldom acknowledge this. Sometimes universities shift money from other areas to operate equipment and buildings that in the first instance were not high priorities.

Major donations seldom augment general university revenues. They generally bolster specific ongoing activities, reorient ongoing activities, and launch new initiatives. But the pressing need is always for operating revenues for salaries; for renovations and physical plant maintenance, notably student common space; for telephones and computers; and for books and periodicals. These are the very things that determine the quality of undergraduate programs.

Two major problems arise. First, fundraising increases pressure on operating accounts when universities divert money from the ongoing to sustain the new. Second, provincial governments, the prime source of university operating funds, may shift their priorities in response to university fundraising. They may match private donations and reduce the general grant accordingly. Or they can simply look at successful university campaigns and put more money into health care or other pressing public priorities. Either way, universities' financial position is static. Either way, priority setting becomes complex as universities accommodate donors.

Fundraising can help universities when it is thoughtfully considered and carefully allied with university priorities. But it is not a panacea for higher education in Canada. Corporations are not boundless in their generosity or capacity to fund universities. Wealthy institutions and individuals are bombarded by requests for financial assistance from many worthy causes. Universities such as Toronto, McGill, and British Columbia are able to accumulate substantial endowments. But fundraising is a challenge even for such major universities. Canadian governments will remain the principal source of university revenues for the foreseeable future, a point not lost on savvy presidents.

Advertising

Advertising is another aspect of commercialization. It has two dimensions that concern us – the university as advertiser and the university as a site for others' advertising. Turning to the university as advertiser, we note an increase in university advertising and promotion. Senior appointments, major donations, and student accomplishments are advertised in outlets such as the *Globe and Mail* and *National Post*. Universities have brochures that announce "world class" faculty, students, or physical facilities.

Universities promote their medical research. Indeed, a noteworthy feature of CBC and CTV national television news is its frequent coverage of university-based medical science. Such coverage is the result of university public relations experts who know how to attract attention.

Another trend is studies noting the contribution of universities to local economic prosperity. Universities tout their stable of academic all-Canadians, students who excel in intercollegiate sports and scholastics. Universities often sponsor studies of the employability of graduates and student satisfaction with their education. The former routinely show that stable employment and high incomes flow to university graduates while the latter reveal high levels of student satisfaction. Another common message is that universities are linked with local, national, and international organizations: they are not ivory towers.

What explains universities' emphasis on advertising? Two assumptions are that business leaders want to know about universities and that they are impressed by what they hear. Universities also assert that they must compete for excellent students and that advertising sways applicants. Competition for students is somewhat illusory, as most undergraduate students at Canadian universities commute to campus. They are generally residents of the large cities where most large universities are located. The option of going elsewhere for an undergraduate degree is beyond the means of most Canadian families. Graduate student recruitment is admittedly different. But advertising is unlikely to be influential. Graduate students go to universities with acknowledged expertise in their chosen fields. They learn where the action is from their professors not from university publicity. The deeper assumption is that there is an untapped reservoir of public support for Canadian universities and that advertising will harness it.

Canadian universities are now important sites for corporate advertising. Their washrooms and elevators frequently contain advertising. Corporate logos appear at sports events and buildings. Rooms and wings within buildings are sometimes named after donors. University events are frequently partnered with companies that have commercial interests in university research or in the student body as future employees or consumers.

On-campus advertising can be seen as either inconsequential or simply as a necessary way to communicate with citizens and students. But it raises important issues. By definition advertising tries to heighten and alter expectations. If not carefully conceived, it can lead to spiralling rhetoric about the quality and value of universities. Students, professors, and staff often note gaps between university claims and university reality.

Management Practices

Commercialization extends to the internal management of Canadian universities. At issue is the application of new public management principles to university affairs.[5] New public management is a mix of business management principles, political ideas, and motivational rhetoric. It is influenced by the customer service revolution that has gripped major retail conglomerates in the last two decades. It stresses customer service, results management, and performance measurement. New public management also advocates "alternative service delivery," including privatization, contracting out, and partnerships. It talks about vision statements, employee entrepreneurship, and strategic plans.

New public management principles are widely, albeit unevenly, applied in Canadian universities. All universities now have vision statements, business plans, and "strategic" initiatives. Performance indicators are used for advertising and as decision-making tools. Universities cite data about research grants, academic all-Canadians, and corporate donations as evidence of their quality.

To a degree, new public management practices are learned through interaction with provincial public servants who, especially in Alberta and Ontario, are often strong advocates of its tenets. Provincial governments want universities to do business plans and to employ performance indicators that assist provincial budgeting. New public management's commitment to efficiency and organizational entrepreneurship may also convince business leaders that universities are well run and hence worthy of support. For their part, senior university management may believe that they are advancing their institutions and moving them into line with cutting-edge organizations in the private sector.

Public management theory now asserts that public organizations must decide priorities, establish core businesses, and shed peripheral ones. This dimension of managerialism has an important, but potentially damaging, impact on university priorities. Universities undertake many complex activities. The challenge has always been to determine the purposes of higher education and to establish meaningful criteria for deciding which fields of study and research merit university support. To this end, new public management asks major questions. But it resolves the basic matter of priorities simplistically. Universities may decide important intellectual questions on the basis of narrow, quantifiable economic and financial grounds. Enrolment data, the employability of graduates, and costs of instruction per capita are at best secondary to serious discussions about curriculum, subjects to be taught, and universities' broader obligations. For this reason, critics see managerialism as a fundamental challenge to educational principles.

Student Employability

North American universities have long prided themselves on their relevance to the broader society. Access to good jobs, contacts (now called networks), and upward mobility often motivate students to undertake higher education.[6] At least implicitly, such goals have long been recognized as legitimate by universities themselves. North American universities thrive in societies that prize hustle over reflection and hard knocks over book learning.

Canadian universities now place heavy attention on preparing students for the economy. Almost all programs claim to equip students for employment and to teach them skills and behaviours required for economic success. Universities emphasize internships and cooperative educational programs that provide work experience as part of university study. Such programs claim to give learning a real-world flavour and to link theory and practice. They prepare students for high-paying jobs upon graduation.

Sheila Slaughter observed that all university programs now resemble Masters of Business Administration.[7] In other words, an emphasis on relevance and employability reduces higher education to the acquisition of work-related skills. Moreover, such commercialization has an infectious impact. Students flock to areas where employability is high. Programs with internships or work experiences are particularly popular. Such disciplines as political science, history, and sociology fear irrelevance and offer courses that attract students. Hence, language departments and business faculties combine on programs that prepare entrepreneurs for commerce in Asia and Europe. Political science departments offer courses in "law and politics" that give the illusion of pre-law training.

Commercial Science

Canadian universities now undertake "commercial science," especially in science, engineering, and medicine. Commercial science, or entrepreneurial science as it is sometimes called, is a complex phenomenon whose main dimensions are noted by Sheila Slaughter: "Basic research in graduate universities is in the process of being redefined as entrepreneurial science. Entrepreneurial policy includes the development of university-industry partnerships around shared research agendas, the fostering of technology transfer between universities and the private sector, the growth of university-sponsored incubators for science-related, high-risk businesses, and the fostering of companies that 'spin off' from university-patented research, providing the university with royalty income."[8]

Commercial science is manifest by the growth of industry liaison offices or ILOs on Canadian campuses. ILOs link universities and businesses, promote technology transfer, and encourage professors to seek commercial applications for their research. Other examples of commercial science are campus research parks, which house companies started up by, or otherwise allied to, university research. Canadian universities also have endowed professorships, the incumbents' salaries and/or research costs of which are paid for by external benefactors. Centres for applied industrial research, many with corporate and government support, are noteworthy. Commercial science is a growing part of university research in Canada and the United States, as measured by patents, business-university research partnerships, and sponsored research.

Commercial science claims that universities are major forces in the economy that must be directly engaged in the productive process. The idea is that research-driven innovation propels modern economies. Advocates of commercial science argue that wealth awaits those nations, regions, and cities that link universities, companies, and governments. Some universities now argue that innovation is primarily a local or regional process. They advocate ideas about "region states" and "city states" and often cite the successes of Silicon Valley; Austin, Texas; and the Route 128 loop in Boston where companies and universities interact harmoniously.

Advocates of commercial science demand change in three significant areas. First, universities must shed their concerns about links with corporations. Corporations, far from being perverse influences, must be seen as partners that share the vision of a prosperous future. Second, commercial science urges a revisionist view of research. It claims that traditional distinctions between basic research and applied research are misleading. As *The Economist* puts it, this is odd because "it turns upside down conventional thinking about what sort of science a university is good at. Until recently both governments and economists had a pretty clear view. Innovation was thought to follow a straight line from basic research (conducted mainly in universities) through research and development (conducted mainly by firms) and thence into the wider economy. Now analysts have at least noticed that innovations meander into the economy along a much more circuitous path, and often in a form (such as the content of people's heads) that cannot be codified and is therefore impossible to measure."[9] Finally, commercial science advocates a knowledge revolution, the passage of the industrial economy, and the significance of university research as a cornerstone of national economic prosperity.

Commercial science benefits business, governments, and universities. Business gains influence in university decision making and achieves access to research, which enhances competitiveness and profitability. Governments' embrace commercial science as part of their efforts to shape economies in the face of economic restructuring. Their support of practical university research is cited as evidence of their grasp of new economic fundamentals. Provincial governments in Canada and state governments in the United States admire the claims of commercial science about local economic benefits.

Universities endorse commercial science for several reasons, notably its promise of research funding in the face of declining government support.[10] They sometimes see commercial science as a revenue-generating stream. It is seen as a source of new discoveries that, when commercially viable, can generate badly needed university income.

Commercial science also claims to increase higher education's prestige and to bolster its standing in public opinion by stressing "relevant" university research. Universities also gain political clout through alliances with business.

Drawbacks of Commercial Science

Commercial science challenges the idea of universities as democratic institutions. It is conducted separately from most other university business and with less debate and accountability. Industry liaison offices, research institutes involving private sector moneys, and research agreements between universities and companies are dealt with as business, not scholarly, matters. Commercial science is not part of universities' public records. Its full consequences for scholarship and research are seldom debated openly.

Commercial science increases university bureaucracy. Industry-supported research sometimes raises complex questions of law, especially in relationship to ownership and profit sharing. As already noted, universities incur substantial costs to take care of this business. When things go wrong, lawsuits can result between professors, companies, and governments.

Industry liaison offices have professional staffs, who neither teach nor do research; their exclusive role is to promote technology transfer. The offices of deans of engineering, medicine, and science and vice-presidents of research devote substantial resources to the pursuit, negotiation, and supervision of sponsored research. Their work, especially in health sciences, is complex and often involves negotiations with major companies. Commercial science leads to bureaucratized, legalistic universities, which are then decried by their very architects.

Commercial science can weaken public confidence in universities. Universities' integrity is called into question when professors are funded by the companies (or their rivals) whose very products they are evaluating. Public concerns are heightened when professors provide competing interpretations of the effectiveness of important medicines. The same trend is noteworthy in the debate about genetically modified foods, where claims revolve around whose science is good or bad and which scientists are neutral or biased.

Commercial science leads to alliances between businesses and universities that may distort university priorities and decision making. In their quest for research funds, universities may adopt positions on a range of important public policy matters. In so doing, they may knowingly or unwittingly link themselves with corporations and thereby operate in ways contrary to other legitimate interests and groups in society. In this way, universities can seriously overextend their mandates as educational institutions. Their priorities can be badly distorted as a result.

Industry-sponsored research can also make Canadian universities more secretive. Companies that fund applied research do so for commercial gain and competitive advantage. By its very nature, secret research is contrary to university ideals of open, unbiased inquiry.

The extent of university secrecy in Canada is not well documented but it has been studied in the United States with worrisome results.[11] At American universities, research secrecy is directly related to the extent and closeness of industry sponsorship. Research institutes that develop commercially viable products are more secretive than parts of the university with no such mandate.

The instruments of secrecy are themselves cause for concern. An American survey notes the spread of company-university agreements that allow publication delays as protection of the commercial interests of research sponsors. Less common are agreements that allow sponsors to delete findings, arguments, and conclusions prior to public release. Occasionally, agreements even sanction communication restrictions between researchers at the same university and between researchers at different universities.

Secret research is contrary to the long-term interests of corporations let alone universities. Costly experiments can be duplicated when medical researchers do not interact, share data, and debate conclusions. Moreover, secrecy in research impedes the dialogue through which evidence is assessed, conclusions are compared, and research questions are posed. A review of industry-university relations by Wesley M. Cohen, Richard Florida, Lucien Randazzese, and John Walsh argues that public sites, notably conferences and publications, remain the preeminent forums for university-industry interaction.[12] Secrecy that removes researchers and research results from the public domain are contrary to the promotion of national economic strength, the very goal of commercial science. Secret research may give its sponsors short-term advantage but at the cost of the larger stock of public knowledge, which is the real source of economic and intellectual advance.

Cohen and his colleagues note two obvious solutions. The first is to increase government funding for basic research. Such funding would reduce the need for university-industry partnerships as a source of research funds. The second option is to enforce stronger interuniversity norms about disclosure. In other words, universities would agree that professors could not

undertake sponsored research if it involved unacceptable secrecy. Corporations would have to abide by such rules or do the research themselves.
We take up this question again in Chapter 10.

Secretive campuses are unhappy ones. Universities, already plagued by
rivalries and factionalism, face another challenge as colleagues and students
argue about ownership of ideas. And secret research raises questions about
external distortion of university priorities. Will universities ignore important questions for which funding is not available and whose study might
offend research sponsors? If universities are reluctant to do critical analysis
and to examine ignored questions, who will fill the gap?

THE FUTURE OF THE COMMERCIAL UNIVERSITY

Is commercial science, with its emphasis on marketable research, a water-
shed in the role of the modern research university? Are Canadian universities becoming mere operating extensions of businesses? We acknowledge
the growing significance of commercial science as universities struggle to
claim stakes in the products and processes they develop. And we note the
possible impact on open inquiry. But commercial science has not, and will
not, transform Canadian universities.

In the latter half of the twenty century, governments supported applied
and basic research.[13] Commercial science is part of a long history of mission-
oriented research, although its emphasis on direct university financial benefit from research is a new development. Moreover, basic research is still
the preeminent concern of university-based scientists in North America.
Commercial science may simply reflect greater funding in established areas
of applied research, not a profound redefinition of research.

Advocates and critics of commercial science unanimously root its rise
in the severe government expenditure restraint of the 1980s and 1990s. But
some governments, notably the Government of Canada, are now running
budget surpluses. In postdeficit Canada, substantial increases in government
funding for scientific research are likely. Commercial science, already under
attack, may lose its raison d'être and lustre.

No evidence suggests that university-based scientists in Canada see basic
and applied research as seamless activities. Basic research, inspired by ideals
of open inquiry, remains the dominant theme in scientific inquiry. Basic

research is also seen as the premier training ground for future scientists, a point certainly not lost on those businesses more dependent on universities for trained personnel than for new products and processes.

Commercial science adds new dimensions to higher education's already crowded agenda. It institutionalizes links between governments, firms, and researchers in the development of new products. It highlights the strength of commercially oriented faculties within universities. Commercial science confers power on elements of engineering, computer science, biochemistry, and agricultural sciences that are important for the economy. They are centres of power and influence both on and off campus and can therefore distort decision making.

Readers are reminded of Clark Kerr's depiction of the multiversity, a striking term coined to describe modern research universities.[14] For Kerr, large North American universities embrace many disciplines, programs, and priorities. The multiversity has elements of the German research university, the American land grant college, and the classic English university. Commercial science adds another complex piece that evokes debate about university objectivity, research secrecy and conflicts of interest, and obligation. It adds controversy to modern science and highlights competing priorities within scientific disciplines.

That said, observers of commercial science often exaggerate its radical character and neglect its continuity with long-standing university trends. Both its advocates and its critics see research as the primary function of universities. They differ primarily regarding the emphasis between applied and basic research. Moreover, commercial science is indifferent to teaching. Its rationale lies in arguments about national economic competitiveness and industrial progress. It acknowledges teaching only when it mentions that students may gain work experience doing research on new products and processes. Students are peripheral to commercial science except as employees. In this sense, entrepreneurial science reflects and accelerates the demise of teaching.

Critics worry that commercial trends in universities will pervert hiring and career advancement. Their precise concern is that professors may be required to give evidence of commercial prowess and inclinations. But consider this: even Faculties of Arts at Canadian universities now prize entrepreneurship in the pursuit of research grants. Capacity to raise research money is widely seen as a virtue. Such ideas have roots quite independent of commercial science. They flourish in research universities.

Opponents of commercial science challenge its tolerance, if not promotion, of secrecy. Seldom do they note that secrecy already surrounds scholarly research even in areas without commercial significance. Professors are sometimes reluctant to interact with each other, to share ideas, and to present controversial findings or ideas in preliminary form. They are competitive, publication-driven, and sometimes fearful, not of loss of commercial advantage, but of plagiarism or other forms of academic dishonesty by their colleagues. Canadian universities have controversies about misappropriation of ideas, data, and findings in areas without commercial implications. Such secrecy is informal insofar as it is not sanctioned by contracts or by university practices. But it is secrecy nonetheless.

Critics of commercial forces often lament its adverse impact on Faculties of Arts. To our minds, commercial science reinforces and reflects the hegemony of science on Canadian campuses. It is part of a larger process of university transformation. Second, Faculties of Arts have hastened, if not authored, their own demise. They have downplayed teaching, imitated Faculties of Science, and made claims about the economic significance of their research. For two decades they tried to gain public esteem by emulating Faculties of Science. When they have dared to be different, Faculties of Arts have undertaken specialized research and teaching as society cries out for the big picture.

CONCLUSION

This chapter has reviewed commercial pressures within Canadian universities. It notes soft commercialism, whose principal manifestations are fundraising, advertising, and the application of business principles to university management. Such forces align universities with business, promote a subtle commercial imperative in university activities, and raise questions about the future of Canadian universities as sites for critical analysis.

We also discussed commercial science that sees Canadian universities as producers of goods and services and as economic partners of business. Manifestations of this trend are the growth of university investment in spin-off companies and efforts to promote technology transfer from university labs to markets.

Commercial pressures in Canadian universities have many causes, consequences, and characteristics. As a result, generalizations are difficult. It can certainly be said, however, that commercial science can significantly distort university priorities. For one thing, it gives unwarranted priority to such important but noneducational goals as national economic development and revenue generation. Commercial research compromises university ideals when it is secretive, distorting of research priorities, or driven by financial pressures to arrive at pleasing conclusions to sponsors. Commercial science is unique among university activities in its *explicit* indifference to teaching.

Commercial pressures allow nonuniversity personnel and interests to shape university decision making. They can also lead to unfair power differentials within the university by conferring considerable money on particular faculties, researchers, and programs. University priorities are thus shaped by financial clout not educational principles. Finally, commercial science often bypasses university decision-making processes and can be a form of clandestine government.

The commercial university assumes that higher education must be relevant to society. The quest for relevance is highlighted by universities' stress on the employability of graduates and by their commitment to economic growth through research partnerships with business. Relevance, even if assumed to be an important university priority, is difficult to define precisely. Does relevant research really increase society's esteem for higher education?

Maxine Singer, president of the Carnegie Institution in Washington, reminds us that astronomy, a discipline renowned for its emphasis on the impractical, is the most fascinating scientific endeavour for society at large.[15] It remains in tune with public opinion and clear about its priorities. Astronomy's high stature stands in contrast to other scientific and medical endeavours, which have become distant from society, wracked by ethical conflict, and burdened by an emphasis on practicality.

CHAPTER 9

PSEUDO-PROBLEMS AND PSEUDO-SOLUTIONS

Many supporters of Canadian universities accept the status quo uncritically. For example, they treat the proposition that teaching and research are mutually supportive as an iron law rather than a thesis that requires supporting evidence and argument. However, many who broadly support the status quo also recognize that Canadian universities are imperfect and cry out for reforms – even far-reaching reforms. This chapter argues that commonly advanced reforms are off base either because they address pseudo-problems or because they embody pseudo-solutions or both.[1] Moreover, most common reforms are flawed because they aim to maintain – and in some cases even increase – the preeminence of research as a university priority. We describe briefly the contents and rationales of the leading proposed reforms and then show how they rest on either pseudo-solutions or pseudo-problems.

INTERDISCIPLINARY STUDIES

The strengthening and extension of interdisciplinary studies is a frequently advanced reform of Canadian universities. The argument for this reform is that traditional academic disciplines like botany, history, and English are too confining. Professors have vested interests in the traditional disciplines, which act as blinkers and inhibit fruitful studies of particular problems, or groups, or geographical areas that are not the subject matter of existing disciplines. For example, traditional disciplines are not easily adapted to the study of the ecology of boreal forests, or the conditions and prospects of women, or the many dimensions of life in China. What Canadian universities need is much greater use of *teams* of scholars from different disciplines to engage in more relevant research and teaching. Canadian studies, environmental studies, Native studies, and women's studies are current examples of interdisciplinary programs typically found in Canadian universities. There is allegedly need for more of the same, often without creating new academic departments. To give an example, perhaps the study of immigration would be best served by teaching and research conducted by teams comprising economists, linguists, demographers, physicians, political scientists, historians, and geographers.

The call for more interdisciplinary research and teaching seems innovative, even daring. It seems quite plausible because many professors are narrow specialists. Some professors of medicine know more than enough about "their" disease and too little about anything else. Some economists refuse to take political influences seriously because politics do not fit their science. Some historians neither know nor care about anything other than religion in New England. Narrow specialization of this kind, which treats the borders of established disciplines as though they were electric fences, is widespread and reprehensible.

Calls for more interdisciplinary study are not new. The same call, supported by the same arguments, has been made for over forty years. Yet no major scholarly achievement can be credited to programmatic interdisciplinary work. This is not a persuasive record of achievement. Some proponents of interdisciplinary studies still claim that their ideas have not been tested and failed, but have never been tried. This explanation ignores two problems with the program of proponents of interdisciplinary study.

First, narrow specialization does not follow inescapably from immersion in an established discipline. For example, no law of nature prevents sociologists from taking up broad, important questions that require them to expand their horizons well beyond the (quite fluid) boundaries of their discipline. What now prevents a sociologist from engaging, for example, in a broad comparative study of the treatment of lawbreakers in several societies? As such a study progresses, the sociologist would have to broaden her horizons as her growing knowledge made her aware of her ignorance. She would have to become something of an economist, a philosopher, a historian, an anthropologist, a lawyer, a psychologist and a political scientist. She would also have to become a student of literature, which might require her to acquire competence in foreign languages. Great sociologists have always been more than sociologists. Such renowned sociologists as Durkheim, Marx, and Weber undertook extraordinarily wide-ranging analyses. Most other sociologists will not equal their achievements but they should certainly aspire to their breadth, as most highly regarded sociologists do. Thoughtful practitioners of other disciplines – whether medicine, mathematics, or music – also strive for and achieve competence outside their own disciplines. So the first problem with the program of the interdisciplinarians is that no program is required. What is really required is that scholars reject narrow disciplinary specialization as the best already do.

The second problem with proposals for more interdisciplinary study is that the interdisciplinary study envisioned will probably not overcome narrow specialization. In proponents' view, a study is interdisciplinary if its subject does not fall neatly within the boundaries of an established discipline. Departments of Canadian Studies, Native Studies, and Women's Studies are often seen as successful practitioners of interdisciplinary study. Notice three things about such departments, however. First, the professors in such departments are trained in established academic disciplines. Some readers may object that this is so simply because doctorates are not yet offered in such interdisciplinary fields. However, it is difficult to see how the study of Canadians, or women, or Aboriginal people could constitute a discipline. Second, it is probably true that purportedly interdisciplinary departments stem from the failure of the established disciplines to address effectively the conditions, problems, and prospects of Canadians, women, and Aboriginal people. For example, there would be no need for Departments of Native Studies to give courses on Aboriginal self-government or Departments of Women's Studies to investigate the shortage of women in elite positions in political parties if political scientists had done so.[2] Finally, we find no evidence that the studies undertaken in interdisciplinary departments are broader and less specialized than those undertaken in the established disciplines. Studying the symbols on Sioux moccasins in the nineteenth century or the migration of Métis along the Saskatchewan

River may be interdisciplinary. However, such studies – which are characteristic of the studies undertaken in Departments of Native Studies – do not exceed in breadth, critical bite, or social responsiveness the studies typically conducted by established disciplines. In any case, few of the studies are genuinely interdisciplinary.

Interdisciplinary study is a commendable rejection of blind adherence to the lore of established disciplines. But it is not a panacea. Long advocacy of interdisciplinary study as a program has borne little fruit. More often than not it has been a cover for the now tired professorial project of more research, more specialization, and less attention to students.

TECHNOLOGY

Early in the twenty-first century, the widespread adoption of new technologies for teaching and research is commonly proposed as a major university reform. (For purposes of salesmanship, "new technologies" is the preferred term. In practice, however, all the technologies come down to one: the computer. Talk of technologies simply recognizes that computers have many applications, with many more to come.) It is a misnomer to label technology advocates as reformers. They are thoroughgoing conservatives who simply want to adapt advanced education to new realities.[3] They don't see anything fundamentally wrong with universities as they are; they just don't want them to fall behind.

The conservatism of technology boosters reveals itself in their postulates about the new digital world. Their first postulate is that microchip technology constitutes a system of alternative delivery of postsecondary education. The assumption here is that advanced education is a product that can be conveyed from producer to consumer in a variety of ways without altering the product. Once this postulate is conceded, it is simply a matter of cost-benefit analysis to determine which mode of conveyance is the most efficient. It is a reasonable conclusion, given this assumption, that high-tech delivery is the most efficient.

A second conservative postulate of technology advocates is that universities are in the early stages of an intense competition for eminence and perhaps even for survival. If the issue is choosing and implementing the most efficient mode of delivery of education, inefficient deliverers will be punished by the loss of "customers." Any university that falls far behind in the technological race risks the fate of the buggy-whip manufacturer in the era of the automobile. Moreover, competition is not just among Canadian universities. American universities are already offering distance-education courses online. In addition, a few quasi-universities run along strictly commercial lines have already started up in the United States.[4] If they efficiently satisfy the customer (university students) demand, there is, say technology boosters, nothing to prevent them from supplanting universities.

A third conservative postulate is that citizens are powerless to resist such basic socioeconomic trends as globalization and the information-based economy. These terms are now clichés, so it is impossible to attach precise meaning to them. However, globalization refers broadly to a process whereby all parts of the earth are becoming integrated at an ever-increasing pace. This integration covers many spheres of life but most commentators stress economic globalization. Discussions of globalization invariably centre on the capacity of corporations to act independently of national borders and to shift production from North American and European locations to lower-cost sites around the world.

The information-based economy is closely connected to globalization. The arrival of the global economy means the increasing transfer of old, low-tech, manufacturing industries to "developing countries." This leaves information as the main commodity of developed countries. According to this scenario, for young people today the main opportunities for well-paid employment are in computer-based industries in which information is the principal factor of both production and consumption.

For technology boosters, globalization and the information-based economy have clear implications for higher education. Universities must devote themselves to training students for the world in which they live. This means training in the skills and techniques of information dissemination and retrieval.

Finally, technology boosters believe that the principal task of universities is to prepare students for their role in the economy. This obviously conservative postulate ties together the others. If we see universities primarily as corporations that provide a service in the capitalist market – namely the provision of skilled workers – the other postulates fall nicely into place.

Advanced education is a commodity that can be conveyed from producer to consumer in a variety of ways – the point is to find the most efficient way, which, as it happens, is computer-driven. Since capitalism is a sophisticated but harsh system of competition, it is no surprise that universities are forced into a competition for high-tech supremacy. In an era of globalization and revolutionary transformation of wealthy countries into information-based economies, the obvious task of universities is to produce "human resources" (the label is revealing in its technological reduction of persons into factors of production) who can adeptly use the latest means for processing information.

The postulates described above generate the program for Canadian universities advocated by technology boosters. The seven main components of this program are these:

1. Provide more computer facilities in universities, including ample computer labs for students, connection of all academic and administrative offices to the World Wide Web by fibre-optic cable, and provision of extensive technical assistance in computer use.

2. Require that all students and faculty become computer literate as quickly as possible.

3. Build "smart classrooms" that contain high-speed computer connections at every desk, computer consoles for teachers, and facilities for interface with other universities so that classes meeting at the same time at different universities can communicate with each other.

4. Require that all students in particular faculties (for example, engineering and business) or even entire universities (for example, Acadia) purchase computers to be used in every course.[5]

5. Reward teachers who (a) learn and (b) employ techniques of alternative delivery in their courses.

6. Reward teachers who produce new software for teaching and learning, especially if the software is widely adopted, thereby bringing prestige and profit to the home university.

7. Emphasize that university education is a life-long process. This means that "human resources" should return to the university from time to time during their careers to ensure that their skills are as current as possible.

At this point, we will state the obvious. We do not oppose in principle technological innovation in Canadian universities. Far from it. Technological advances have made advanced education easier and more accessible. As far as we know, no one contests the value of moveable print, the telephone, or audio tapes and videotapes, although everyone acknowledges that these technologies can be overused or used inappropriately. We see no reason for assessing computer technology any differently. Computer-based technology enhances ease and access but it too can be overused or misused. Consider the World Wide Web, which is a vast improvement over other media for disseminating information. As political scientists, we sometimes need information on voting turnout in the last election in Newfoundland, or the gross national product of African countries north of the Sahara, or the platform of the Australian Labor Party. Such information can be quickly accessed on the Web, eliminating the need for lengthy library searches through newspapers, periodicals, and government documents. On a day-to-day basis, computer technology has made university libraries infinitely easier to use and much more accessible. That said, the Web does not score well for conveying subtle shades of meaning. It is nearly hopeless as a medium for serious dialogue. As with other technology, advanced computer technology has major strengths and weaknesses that must constantly be borne in mind.

Astonishingly, technology boosters have learned little from the overselling of television as an educational medium in the 1960s. In those days, even before satellite transmission and videotape, enthusiasts forecast a technological revolution in higher education with the optimism and ardour of today's computer advocates. In the United States, plans were made to telecast lectures simultaneously to dozens of colleges and universities from television studios in airplanes circling overhead. The idea was to save money and to ensure that lectures were given by photogenic and charismatic speakers. Some reformers even suggested that professors should write scripts to be delivered by celebrities: The Ed Sullivan Calculus Show and The Marilyn Monroe Epistemology Hour. Technology boosters invariably forget, however, that university education is not about passive consumption of information or the ideas of brilliant professors.

Technology advocates advance two pseudo-problems. The first pseudo-problem is, How can universities carry out most efficiently their principal task of preparing students for their roles in the modern economy, an economy dominated by the immutable forces of globalization and endless innovation in the processing of information? The second pseudo-problem is, How can Canadian universities best compete in a technological war with each other, with American universities and with quasi-university corporations?

The first "problem" is false even if globalization and the growth of the information-processing economy are unstoppable forces (which we doubt). It is false because the main task of universities is not job preparation. This is certainly one of the tasks of universities (and always has been). But universities have many other important tasks, including disinterested contemplation of nature, cultivation of aesthetic sensibilities, broadening of appreciation of histories and cultures, sharpening capacities for philosophical analysis and synthesis, and refinement of practical reason. If any one task of universities is the principal one (because it is indispensable to all others), it is the cultivation of the critical attitude that leads us to replace worse beliefs with better ones.

The second pseudo-problem is how to succeed in the competition among universities and between universities and quasi-university educational institutions. Upon reflection, the underlying assumption of this pseudo-problem is remarkably crass. The assumption is that Canadian universities should do whatever it takes to maintain or, better, increase their market share of students. We see how crass this assumption is when we recognize that there are better (and much cheaper) ways for Canadian universities to increase market share than to enter the computer rat race. American state universities provide models for two ways to increase market share. One is to hire many more professors of business and then allow students in other faculties to take degrees with a large business component. As technology advocates recognize, many university students are heavily career-oriented. Wider availability of business-preparation programs would be an attraction for them. If necessary, universities could cover the cost of hiring more business professors by cutting "frills" such as classics, fine arts, and philosophy. A second method of recruitment that Canadian universities could borrow from American state universities is the addition of gut courses and programs. ("Gut" is American slang for courses that require little time and effort.) Thus, for example, Canadian universities could provide courses analyzing television soap operas and talk shows, and degrees in sports communications. Indeed, as soon as we accept the market share perspective, we open up a host of opportunities for student recruitment by Canadian universities. An obvious avenue is to plunder our own technical institutes and community colleges. Plenty of young people would take a university degree in cosmetology, spot welding, or landscaping. Technology boosters, with their constant reference to postsecondary education, with its implication that the allocation of tasks among advanced educational institutions is simply a bureaucratic matter, can have no principled objection to this method of recruitment. But all this is silly. The assumption that universities should do whatever is required to maximize their market share – whether that be competing for eminence in computer gadgetry or providing courses in designing schedules for softball tournaments – is crass and stupid. If the careful use of computer technology for worthwhile university purposes leads some Canadian students to opt for flashier American universities or corporations, so be it! Canadian universities cannot improve themselves by selling their souls.

Technology boosters present two pseudo-solutions. The first is that computer technology is simply the most efficient means of alternative delivery of a product. The second is that the best way to improve teaching is to reward teachers who develop and implement technologically sophisticated teaching techniques.

The idea that computer technology solves a problem of efficient delivery of an educational product presupposes (a) that university education is a product and (b) that it is possible to deliver this product in a variety of ways without significantly altering its character. Technology boosters *assert* these claims rather than defend them with evidence and argument. Both claims are wildly implausible. The idea that a course on Shakespeare's sonnets is the same product whether it is delivered by lecture, seminar, book, telephone, audio tape, videotape, or Web page strains credulity to the breaking point. Some readers may object to the example of a course on Shakespeare's sonnets, arguing that fairer examples are courses in descriptive statistics or German grammar. We don't believe that it is possible to produce courses even on statistics or grammar that remain the same regardless of how they are delivered, in such a way that the sole issue is efficiency. However, for the sake of argument let us suppose that this is possible, since our main point is obvious in any case. If it is possible to produce and deliver courses in statistics more or less efficiently but not possible to do so for a course in Shakespeare's sonnets, the claim of technology advocates that computer technology solves a problem of efficient delivery of a product is false. The most that can be said is that some courses (or, more likely, some parts of some courses) can be taught more effectively, or as effectively but more cheaply, with computer technology. We apologize for taking so long to make the obvious point that the appropriate attitude toward technology in university education is both welcoming and critical. Widespread technology boosterism demands that we belabour the obvious.

The other pseudo-solution is that the best way to improve teaching is to reward teachers who adopt – or, better, invent – technologically advanced teaching methods. This is a pseudo-solution because poor teaching in universities is not mainly a problem of technique but of motivation. Young professors find out quickly that rewards are for research not for teaching. As a result, many of them put as little time as possible into teaching. To the extent that universities wish to use rewards to improve teaching, they should reward *good* teaching regardless of its style. In some cases, good teaching will involve the adoption or creation of computer-based techniques. More often, it will require a basic change in attitude and an attempt to master traditional teaching methods.

We therefore make two unremarkable conclusions about the increased use of computer-based technology for teaching and research in Canadian universities. First, universities should maintain an open but critical attitude toward computer technology. Some of it is undoubtedly an improvement, but much of it is not. Second, uncritical technology boosters vastly exaggerate the benefits of computer-based education.

TWO TYPES OF PROFESSORS

Some commentators maintain that many university problems would be solved by creating two categories of professors: teaching professors and research professors. This measure appears to address the problem that some professors have a greater aptitude and inclination to teach than others, who are more suited to research. We begin by treating it as though it were intended as a solution to a problem, and we argue that it is pseudo-solution.

However, we also show that there is a deeper difficulty with the proposal: it deals with a pseudo-problem.

A few professors excel both as frontier researchers and as teachers. But such paragons are a small minority. Most professors have greater – and sometimes much greater – strengths in one activity or the other. The resulting problem is that strong researchers tend to be weak teachers and strong teachers tend to be weak researchers. The change would be advantageous to both students and professors. Students would be exposed only to very good and very committed teachers, and professors would be able to do what they do best. However, reflection reveals that the solution is actually a pseudo-solution.

An initial problem with the two categories proposal is that it contradicts a central tenet of Canadian universities – that good teaching and good research go hand in hand and are mutually reinforcing. If good teaching and good research were inseparable, it would solve nothing to separate them. In fact, it would be a disaster. This contradiction doesn't sink the two categories proposal, however, since the mutual reinforcement thesis is unproven and almost certainly false. The two categories proposal addresses a pseudo-problem.

Larger problems arise. As we have stressed, research is currently regarded as far more important than teaching. It is inevitable that the division between categories of professors would also be a division between classes of professors (probably involving differences of pay as well as prestige). Given a choice, most professors, including those whose strong suit is teaching, would opt to be research professors. In practice, teaching professors would be those who couldn't make the grade.

The two categories system also ignores the fact that there is a third category: sessional lecturers. There is a very real possibility – actually a high probability – that the actual division would be: (1) research professors, (2) teaching professors conducting small, advanced courses and writing as much as possible in order to secure their promotion to research professor, and (3) sessional lecturers, doing the bulk of demanding teaching, with little opportunity to do research even if that is their natural bent.

The two categories proposal seems to be a pseudo-solution to a real problem: the problem that some professors shine at research and others at teaching. However, deeper analysis reveals that the problem is itself a pseudo-problem. It is a pseudo-problem because it rests on a destructively narrow conception of research as exclusively frontier, fact-finding research and teaching as some kind of skill or gift divorced from deep thought. An indispensable requirement for all professors, whether they are most at home conducting experiments in molecular biology or teaching introductory Mandarin, is an aptitude for, and commitment to, reflective inquiry. Reflective inquiry infuses both teaching and research. Researchers who are insufficiently reflective to teach and teachers who are insufficiently reflective to do research are incompetent to be professors. They should not be hired as professors, and if inadvertently hired, they should be dismissed. The proposal to create two categories of professors addresses a pseudo-problem.

HARVARD(S) OF THE NORTH

Another popular scheme for reforming Canadian universities is to create one or more Canadian replicas of a prestigious American university. The assumption is that even the best Canadian universities are far inferior to the best American ones, such as Harvard, Princeton, Chicago, and Stanford. (Interestingly, such prestigious American universities seem little interested in computer technology.) If Canada is to play in the big leagues of international higher education, we need one or more world-class universities of the calibre of Yale or Columbia. These universities are relatively small and very rich. They can afford internationally renowned professors in all fields. They can be very selective in the students they admit. Excellent students apply from all over the world, and these universities admit only the best. In addition, because these universities are so wealthy, they can assign professors a very light teaching load, which means that their professors produce a great deal of high-quality research. Finally, these prestigious and wealthy universities have a much larger proportion of graduate students than other American universities and, of course, Canadian universities.

Three different schemes for creating one or more Harvards of the North present themselves. The least realistic option is to create an entirely new university that would be a genuine Harvard of the North. Located in or near Canada's major city, Toronto, and very generously funded, it would attract outstanding professors and students and produce outstanding research.

Somewhat more realistic is the proposal to recognize that the University of Toronto is now the best Canadian university. The Harvard of the North scheme suggested by this fact is to make it even better. To achieve this end, the University of Toronto should reduce teaching loads, gradually replace its least productive professors with world-class researchers, and significantly increase the ratio of graduate to undergraduate students.

The most realistic proposal is to create not a single replica of Harvard but a whole Ivy League of research-intensive universities. None of these would quite match Harvard but all would be better than any existing Canadian university and the system as a whole would be much improved if not world class. This proposal requires us to recognize that the existing Canadian research universities are different in kind from those that emphasize undergraduate education or treat research and teaching approximately equally. Governments and private donors should grant the big universities that emphasize research, especially in their large medical schools, more funds to concentrate on new discoveries and the training of graduate students. The Universities of British Columbia, Alberta, Western Ontario, McMaster, Toronto, Queen's, Montreal, McGill, Laval, and Dalhousie should be explicitly recognized as a class of universities in their own right.

The first alternative is unrealistic. First, in an era of financial stringency, governments are most unlikely to look with favour on the creation of a new university. To do so would be extremely expensive because a world-class university needs not only world-class professors but also world-class facilities of all kinds. Second, to have the requisite drawing power, the new university would have to be near Toronto. This means (short of a national effort) that the Government of Ontario would have to fund it, and recent Ontario governments have prided themselves on their thrift. Finally, the University of Toronto, long convinced of its own preeminence, would vigorously oppose the creation of a competitor explicitly designed to excel it. It would be a formidable lobbying force against the creation of such a competitor.

The somewhat more realistic proposal to make the University of Toronto itself Canada's Harvard also faces major obstacles. Here again, the Government of Ontario would look askance at the financial burden. Other Ontario universities – especially the other major research-universities, such as McMaster, Queen's, and Western Ontario – would object forcefully. In any case, the University of Toronto, Canada's largest university by far, is too big, and too heavily "burdened" by the education of undergraduates, to really emulate Harvard.[6]

The idea of creating a miniature replica of the Ivy League, instead of concentrating on the creation of one great university, is (with some modifications) quite realistic. The Universities of British Columbia, Alberta, Western Ontario, McMaster, Toronto, Queen's, Montreal, and McGill already constitute a special class.[7] They lead in emphasizing research over teaching; they receive far more research grants than other universities; they have strong Faculties of Medicine, Natural Science, and Engineering; and they train the overwhelming majority of graduate students. All that is needed is for provincial governments to recognize the need for elite universities. Then they could increase their financial support for the major research universities. They could do this by simply giving more money to the major research universities or by shifting priorities somewhat away from the smaller, less research-intensive universities. Admittedly, the result would not be a real Ivy League of wealthy private universities. There would be no Columbia or University of Pennsylvania let alone a Harvard or Princeton. But there would be a collection of superb universities stretching from sea to sea. The reformed Canadian elite universities would be on a par with the best American state universities. Toronto and McGill would be as good as California and Michigan, and the other members of the big ten would be as good as the universities that make up the American Big Ten, such as Illinois, Wisconsin, Minnesota, and Ohio State.

This third proposal, we suggest, is realistic and meritorious in some ways. But again we note a pseudo-problem and a pseudo-solution. The pseudo-problem is the need for a world-class university on the model of Harvard or, at least, the University of Michigan. What is this need? The label "world class" originated, and is most at home, in athletics. A sprinter is world class only if she can give the world's fastest a run for her money. Canada produces world-class hockey and synchronized swimming teams but not world-class basketball and soccer teams. So what? Why should you care? Even if you do care, why should Canadian governments spend large amounts of money to produce basketball teams that can compete with the Americans and soccer teams that can compete with the Brazilians?

Consider now universities. What is a world-class university? Presumably it is one very much like Harvard. What are the distinctive characteristics of Harvard? It is a rich, private university, which is to say that a large part of its wealth is independent of government generosity or lack thereof. It has a great library. In almost every subject area it has excellent scholars. A high proportion of the student body consists of graduate students. The number of students per professor is very low. Published research is far more important than teaching. Professors do little undergraduate teaching. Some undergraduate teaching is of very poor quality. Above all, professors at other English-language universities *say* that Harvard is world class.

What problem does Harvard address that would justify the huge expenditure required to create a Harvard of the North? Or an Ivy League of the North? Or a Big Ten of the North? The biggest problem Harvard (or the second- and third-best alternatives) solves is the absence of Harvard. Without a Harvard of the North, Canada doesn't have a Harvard. And without the second- and third-best alternatives, it doesn't have even a near-Harvard. For many university professors, the problem that would be solved by creating a Harvard of the North is precisely the absence of a Harvard of the North. Canada, they believe, doesn't have a university that is really excellent. Our best universities are very good but even the best of them allocate too much time and money to teaching undergraduates (often poorly prepared or poorly motivated ones at that) and too little on outstanding research.

On first hearing, this sounds like a compelling argument. Surely there is everything to be said for striving for excellence and nothing to be said against it. Moreover, university education in particular is a realm in which Canada should compete with the best. But upon examination, we see that this is an assertion, not an argument at all. Advocates of a Harvard of the North simply state that (1) a wealthy university with (2) a high proportion of graduate to undergraduate students whose professors are (3) distinguished scholars who (4) devote the bulk of their time to research defines excellence for universities. We have devoted much of this book to refuting this idea of university excellence. We have argued that universities should be judged primarily by the quality of undergraduate education they provide.

Even if the creation of a Harvard of the North (or some close facsimile) were not a pseudo-problem (the false problem of achieving American-style excellence in Canada), it would be a pseudo-solution. That is, even if we granted that a Harvard of the North would be better than any existing Canadian university, the creation of a Canadian Harvard would not significantly improve the quality of university education in Canada. If we are seriously concerned about the quality of university education in Canada as compared with its American counterpart, we have to look at the entire system of university education here and there. When we do this, we find that Harvard educates only a minuscule fraction of American university students. The picture changes hardly at all if we include the rest of the Ivy League, or all the prestigious private universities, or even the state universities that award significant numbers of advanced degrees. Most American university students attend large universities, predominantly urban, that bear no trace of ivy. Like their Canadian counterparts, most American students commute to universities in their hometown (a large or small city or its suburbs). Many of these universities are poorly equipped, overcrowded, and understaffed. Many American universities are mediocre or worse by any credible standard. They are certainly not of Harvard's calibre. As in most comparisons between Canada and the United States, we find that Americans are considerably more willing to make room for the advantages that accrue to superior ability and luck. Although it is true that Canadian universities are defective in many respects, almost all Canadian universities provide a decent education. Many American universities do not. We maintain that it would be unwise and unjust to deprive Canadian universities – that is, their students – to create some version of a Harvard, an Ivy League, or a Big Ten of the North. It would be unwise because it would reduce the overall quality of the Canadian university system, which is in any case none too great. And it would be unjust because, since most students cannot afford to travel far from home to attend university, it would discriminate without good reason against students far away from the universities chosen for preferential treatment.

ABOLITION OF TENURE

Almost no reformer sees abolition of tenure as a cure-all for Canadian universities. However, many observers maintain that it would be a worthwhile reform that would produce noticeable improvements. Most critics of tenure think that professors get a free ride: with tenure they get job security that they retain even if they become lazy or incompetent. Let's remind ourselves of the main characteristics of the institution of tenure, since much of the steam behind the objections to it disappears when we understand it.[8] (Recall our discussion of fictional professor Wayne Young in Chapter 3.)

When professors are hired, they are normally appointed at the rank of assistant professor. This appointment is a probationary one of (usually) five years. In the final year of this probationary term, a group of tenured colleagues investigates carefully the assistant professor's performance and promise over the five years of probation.[9] If this group decides that the assistant professor has shown the requisite ability and motivation and will probably continue to do so, he is granted "appointment without definite term," that is, tenure. Tenure means that the professor is no longer on probation. In the ordinary course of events, he will not be required again to demonstrate his basic competence. The term of his appointment is now unlimited not probationary. Tenure does not mean that the professor cannot be fired. Tenure does not license a professor to retire unofficially while still drawing pay, to use his classroom as a pulpit, or to insult or harass students, colleagues, or administrators. These are all firing offences, tenure or no tenure. Furthermore, almost all universities now have provisions to eliminate professors who are "redundant." If there is practically no demand for courses in ancient Greek, professors of Greek can be discharged even if their performance is satisfactory.

People find tenure objectionable for two reasons. First, our description of tenure is somewhat misleading. As a matter of black-letter law, universities can fire professors whose performance has become grossly inadequate. In practice, tenured professors enjoy so many legal and political protections that university officials are reluctant to try to dismiss them except in extreme cases. So there is some truth in the claim that tenure protects professors who have become deadwood. Second, people find tenure objectionable because few workers, either in the private sector or the public, now have anything like the job security enjoyed by professors. Downsizing is widespread, and highly competent, middle-aged professionals often feel its sting. Critics of tenure ask a legitimate question: Why don't professors accept their fair share of economic insecurity?

These reasons for abolishing tenure are not overwhelmingly powerful. However, they are strong enough that they should carry the day unless the reasons in favour of tenure are strong enough to override them. What is the purpose of tenure? Its purpose is to promote free inquiry by preventing universities from firing professors who reach unpopular conclusions. For example, the Roman Catholic Church might pressure a university to get rid of a theologian who concluded that the Church should consecrate gay marriages. Timber companies might call for the head of a professor who argued that their cutting practices are harmful to wildlife.

Free inquiry in universities is certainly desirable for two reasons that have little to do with the well-being of professors. First, it is the best method of replacing worse views with better ones. Only if we are able to follow evidence and argument wherever they lead us can we exchange current opinions for better ones (or, at best, the truth). Second, free inquiry is the best guarantee that students will be exposed to a wide variety of attitudes, beliefs, and opinions. If professors have a right to free inquiry, they are likely to reach different conclusions, and students will benefit from thinking about, debating, and deciding who is (more nearly) right.

Unfortunately, even the strong case for free inquiry does not settle the issue of tenure. The issue remains because it is easy to design renewable limited-term contracts for professors (say, five years) that would prohibit termination on other than specified academic or moral grounds, which is basically the situation of assistant professors. The logic of this position is powerful. The right of free inquiry should be guaranteed to assistant professors as much as to associate professors (the same reasons apply in both cases), and by and large it is, without tenure. Therefore, tenure is unnecessary.

However, another powerful argument underpins the case for tenure. The argument is that the principal threat to free inquiry now comes not from politicians, or preachers, or business leaders but from professors themselves. Professors in Faculties of Arts, which are the locus of concern about tenure, are now divided into schools of thought that, for the most part, do not engage in dialogue with each other. (To name but a few, classical liberals and neo-liberals, feminists and cultural conservatives, Marxists and post-Marxists, realists and idealists, postmodernists and postindustrialists.) Most of the time, members of these schools coexist in an atmosphere of resentful toleration. However, when personnel decisions are to be made, the superficial comity sometimes disappears. On questions of hiring, giving, or withholding tenure, or granting or denying rewards, the gloves come off. Bad blood between various schools already causes some fierce battles and without doubt some serious injustices as weak professors with the "right" views are rewarded and strong professors with "wrong" views are penalized. There is a very real danger that a system of renewable contracts would lead to unwarranted terminations allegedly on academic grounds but actually on grounds of allegiance to the "wrong" school. Almost as bad, and even more likely, is that many professors would avoid inquiries and opinions that might give offence, retreating to the safety of bland specialization.[10]

Finally, the abolition of tenure would probably lead to an even greater emphasis on research compared with teaching. With five-year periods between contract renewals, the temptation to concentrate even more narrowly on research "productivity" would be practically irresistible. The abolition of tenure would further distort already distorted priorities.

STRENGTHENING LEADERSHIP

As noted in our discussion of the Fabrikant case in Chapter 7, the investigation by management consultant John Scott Cowan found that an important factor in the tragedy was the lack of management skills on the part of Concordia administrators.[11] Cowan saw as the main problem that academic administrators enter professorial careers in which success is performance in research and teaching rather than administrative leadership. His view is that academic leaders are too steeped in professorial ways, and far too inclined to live and let live, to ignore problems, to excuse bad behaviour as eccentricity, and to avoid confrontation until it is too late. As a result, he maintained, those occupying positions of leadership in universities should be required to undergo training in administration.

Cowan is somewhat unusual in recommending that university administrators should be as tough as the toughest chief executive officers of major corporations. However, he is not unusual in seeing improvement in the quality of university executives as a major reform that might be undertaken by Canadian universities. Nowadays almost all advertisements for positions in university government at the rank of dean or higher solicit people who will exercise "strong academic leadership."

We should ask, "What is 'strong academic leadership?'" and "What problem or problems is it supposed to solve?" Strong academic leadership now seems to embrace two types of qualities. The first type falls under the heading of professional competence. A strong academic leader has had previous experience in administration. She is willing and able to make tough (and, if necessary, unpopular) decisions without flinching. The second type of quality of a strong academic leader falls under the heading of persuasive innovation. A strong academic leader must have a clear vision of a golden future for the university. She should be able to convince her associates that they should adopt the realization of this vision as their mission.

What problem or problems is strong academic leadership supposed to solve? Presumably, strong academic leadership qualities of the first type are supposed to solve a problem of amateurism – a lack of experience and skill in handling day-to-day problems. In contrast, strong academic leadership qualities of the second type try to solve a problem of lack of direction or, worse, aimlessness. These ideas embody pseudo-problems and pseudo-solutions.

As we noted in Chapter 7, academic administrators in Canadian universities are not amateurs. For example, a serious contender for appointment as president of a Canadian university should not be much older than fifty. Two five-year terms are the norm, and there is a widespread belief that administrators lose vigour and sharpness after sixty. To be a genuine contender, a candidate must have served at least one (five-year) term as a vice-president who, with some exceptions, has been dean. In turn, a dean often comes from the ranks of chairs of departments (another five-year term). Thus, serious candidates for the presidency of Canadian universities typically have served at least fifteen years as administrators by the age of fifty. That is, they have been administrators since approximately the age of thirty-five – not long after they earned their doctoral degrees. This means that Canadian university administrators are seldom inexperienced amateurs. They have been administrators for most of their working lives. Second, they are not absent-minded professors who stumble into academic administration by accident. They decide to become administrators very early in their careers. Thus, insofar as "strong academic leadership" deals with a problem of administrative amateurism in the universities, it addresses a pseudo-problem. Canadian university administrators are not amateurs.

The second element of "strong academic leadership," persuasive innovation, is supposed to solve the problems of aimlessness and lack of clear university direction. By bringing to their jobs a vision of a better university, and by convincing their associates to adopt this vision, strong academic leaders provide coherence to divided universities. Far-sighted leaders replace disunity, a bad thing, with teamwork, a good thing.

Is there evidence that those with a significant voice in the direction of Canadian universities believe that universities suffer from lack of vision or that disorder should be replaced by teamwork? On these questions, the silence of leading constituencies – administrators, students, and professors – is deafening. Moreover, the visions and missions of Canadian universities are strikingly similar. All strong academic leaders envision a university characterized by excellence. Not surprisingly, all Canadian universities want to be excellent. Excellence is never defined clearly enough that anyone could fail a mission.[12] To the extent that it is given content, excellence is dealt with in terms of reputation. That is, a university is said to be excellent if other people, specifically other people with the mission of creating excellent universities, say it is. This has approximately the same validity as saying that Rita MacNeil is an excellent singer if most Nova Scotians over the age of fifty say so. Even if Canadian universities suffer from a problem of disunity, "strong academic leadership" is not the solution to it.

In summary, insofar as strong academic leadership is understood as addressing a problem of amateurism on the part of Canadian university administrators, it addresses a pseudo-problem. They are not amateurs. Insofar as it is understood as the solution to a problem of disunity, it is a pseudo-solution. No matter how deeply they are committed to a vision, university leaders cannot cause major changes in their institutions without the support of their constituencies, especially the professors. That support is seldom forthcoming.

GREATER RELIANCE ON MARKETS

A hallmark of our times is remarkable confidence in the ability of markets to promote well-being. This confidence is widespread in Canadian universities. We have already considered two proposed reforms that rely heavily on market considerations. One is the call for a stronger commitment to computer-based technology, which rests partly on the supposed need for universities to compete in the market for students and partly on the supposed desirability of preparing students for labour markets. The other is the call for the abolition of tenure. The alleged problem with tenure is that it guarantees job security for the productive and unproductive alike. The market would provide necessary discipline by rewarding the able and industrious and eliminating deadwood.

Several other proposals aim to make universities more like corporations or to subject them more fully to market discipline or both. Among these proposals are the following:

- Universities should engage much more extensively in co-op education in which students spend part of the year in the classroom and part of it working for a firm in their subject of specialization. A program of this kind has long flourished in the Faculty of Engineering at the University of Waterloo, and several other universities have emulated it. Such programs (besides assuring that students do not incur heavy debts) teach students practical applications of their subject. As a result, students become effective employees more quickly than if their training had been entirely academic.

- Governments should provide students, upon completion of high school, with educational vouchers that would enable them to pay for education at any institution they choose (providing that they meet its standards). This would force postsecondary institutions, including universities, to provide the kind of education students want, since unsatisfied demands would bring more competitive providers of education into the market.

- Thought should be given to the creation of for-profit institutions to compete with publicly funded universities. Many students lack interest in theoretical analysis and speculation. They want to live productively and comfortably in the world as it is. They have no need of professors with doctoral degrees from prestigious universities. They would be happier and better served if their teachers were men and women who were successful practitioners of their occupations. Teaching after their regular working hours, these practitioners could provide students with a more relevant and cheaper education than a conventional university.

Proposals to have universities rely more heavily on markets have as their main purpose to better prepare students for the workforce.[13] Rather than take up these proposals one by one, we concentrate on their common theme. Do these proposals address a real problem? Do Canadian universities give their students too little vocational preparation?

This suggestion seems far-fetched. It is especially unconvincing regarding the largest universities. Although the Faculties of Arts and Science are by far the largest in these universities, the professional faculties are also major forces. Large Canadian universities already have Faculties of Business, Education, Engineering, Household Economics, Law, Pharmacy, and more than one faculty in health science (dentistry, medicine, nursing, rehabilitation medicine). Typically, they also have one or more of agriculture, architecture, forestry, journalism, social welfare, and veterinary medicine. Faculties of extension in these universities devote considerable effort to courses devoted to success in careers.

Criticism of the professional faculties for alleged failure to attend to the vocational prospects of their students is rare. The one seeming exception is the Faculty of Education. Professors of education are routinely condemned for filling their students' heads with cuckoo theories of teaching and learning. When the students become teachers, they then act on the cuckoo theories. The result is that our kids can't read, write, or do arithmetic. However, the Faculty of Education is not really an exception to the generalization that people seldom criticize professional faculties for their inattention to the world of work. People who say that professors of education fill students with wacky ideas are not saying that these professors are unconcerned with the students' vocations. The real problem, in their view, is that the professors succeed all too well in influencing the professional lives of their students.

If there is a problem regarding lack of vocational preparation, then, it must be in the Faculties of Arts and Science. Is there a problem in these faculties? To begin with, consider the respects in which there is certainly not a problem:

- Many courses in science, such as those in computing science and meteorology, have direct vocational applications.
- Many science courses are required for the professional faculties.

Engineers need mathematics and physics, and, depending on the type of engineering, some astronomy, chemistry, or geology. Students in the health sciences need courses in biology, chemistry, genetics, and psychology.

- Contrary to common opinion, courses in the fine arts (art, drama, and music) are often heavily vocational. Students in fine arts spend most of their time practising their arts not thinking about them. Well-paying jobs in the fine arts are few but this is not the fault of universities.
- The study of English, insofar as it enables one to read intelligently and write well, is certainly important for most vocations.
- The same is true of the study of (living) languages other than English, as should be obvious to advocates of economic globalization.
- Many social science courses are important for vocations. For example, corporations and governments employ many economists. Many organizations employ political science graduates as political advisors.
- Like Faculties of Science, Faculties of Arts present courses for professional faculties. For example, Faculties of Social Welfare require their students to take courses in sociology. Law schools admit students only after they have acquired the rudiments of a general education, usually in arts. Education students must take courses in the subjects they plan to teach.

In summary, Faculties of Arts and Science already teach a lot of courses with clear vocational benefits. However, they also offer many courses, and faculty members engage in many studies, that are not directly relevant to future employment. Professors of French think and teach about Voltaire, Diderot, and Rousseau, major eighteenth-century French thinkers whose immediate relevance is not obvious. Mathematicians invent alternative geometries that may have no practical bearing in the solar system let alone the Canadian job market. Philosophers continue to discuss questions about the relationship between the mind and the body – including the question of whether this is really a question! – apparently mindless of the impertinence of this issue to investment banking. This stuff is surely nonvocational to the point of being anti-vocational.

Or is it? Take the example of eighteenth-century French literature. If we live in an era of globalization, employment opportunities with organizations that have close relationships with francophone countries will increase. Of course, Canadians who enter these relationships will require fluency in French. However, they will also require considerable knowledge of the history, economics, and culture of these countries. (If you find this claim at all doubtful, consider how you would react to a francophone salesperson, speaking excellent, grammatical English, to whom the names John A. Macdonald, Louis Riel, Margaret Laurence, and Wayne Gretzky meant nothing.) The upshot of this observation is that it would be very difficult to show that courses in (for example) Balkan history, family structures in east Africa, or eighteenth-century French philosophers do nothing to prepare students to make a living.

Consider now the philosophy course on the relationship between mind and body. Let us suppose (what is doubtful) that such a course gives neither a direct nor a (reasonably demonstrable) indirect advantage to the typical job seeker. However, we make two points about this observation. First, there are atypical job seekers and atypical jobs. Some students want to be philosophy teachers. Some want to write for the few magazines that do not require:

Simple-minded.
Very short.
Sentences and paragraphs.
With few verbs.

Some seek other unconventional jobs including jobs that decry the dreariness of many conventional jobs. Second, the philosophy course (if well taught) encourages careful, critical thinking. People in charge of hiring in both the private and the public sectors often say that employees with critical skills and dispositions are required in a rapidly changing world. Admittedly, they often belie their own words by hiring business school graduates rather than philosophy graduates. Still, the case for hiring some people with a sharp critical acumen, who doubt conventional beliefs, who are dissatisfied with the way things are done now, is overwhelming.

We are not arguing that every (and every imaginable) university course contributes to a student's employability. We simply hold that every good course should contribute to a student's employability. But not every course is good. Many courses simply provide information or broadcast the lore of a discipline. They neither involve nor encourage the exercise of the higher intellectual faculties. Even worse, some courses take up unduly narrow topics, usually dictated by the teacher's research agenda rather than students' needs. Such courses discourage synthetic and critical thinking. Finally, as we have often stressed, many courses are taught indifferently by professors who know that the road to success has nothing to do with teaching.

Every good course should contribute to a student's employability. Some courses are not good. As well, some good courses do not impress employers. Andrea may have devoted her undergraduate career to challenging courses, superbly taught. However, if many of these courses aren't snappy enough (Plato's Early Dialogues, The Philosophy of Mathematics, Ancient Physics), or are too snappy (Feminist Ethics, Anarchism, Buddhist Cosmology) employers may lose interest. They may lose interest quickly if the alternative to Andrea is Alice, who concentrated on "safe," uninspiring courses in computing science, physics, and economics, with a geographical focus on the history and culture of her home province. Employers may prefer Alice to Andrea but this does not necessarily show that Andrea's courses were less suited to a vocation. It may show more about the excessive caution and lack of imagination of employers than about the failings of universities.

The case for universities to rely more heavily on markets is unconvincing. The core of that case is that Canadian universities currently do too little to prepare their students for a vocation. This case is largely unfounded. The majority of students in larger universities is in professional faculties that are thoroughly vocational in orientation. Faculties of Arts and Science provide many service courses for the professional faculties. Moreover, good arts and science courses always give students the opportunity to strengthen their ability and inclination to think carefully, critically, and imaginatively. These are qualities that employers say they want. The only courses that do not prepare students for a vocation are bad ones. Most bad courses are bad because they deal with a professor's narrow research interests and are taught casually by a professor who cares more about research than teaching. No university should need the market to teach it that bad courses should be eliminated.

CONCLUSION

Most people who care about Canadian universities say – or, more often, imply by their silence – that universities are basically sound. Nevertheless, most of these supporters allow that there is room for improvement. Some of them propose reforms, even seemingly radical reforms. In this chapter we have examined seven common reforms:

- to expand interdisciplinary studies
- to make much greater use of computer-based technology
- to have two categories of professors – research professors and teaching professors
- to create a Harvard of the North (or several of them)
- to abolish tenure
- to strengthen the leadership of universities
- to rely more heavily on markets.

Such reforms either address a pseudo-problem or propose a pseudo-solution or both. In previous chapters, we have argued that contemporary Canadian universities are seriously flawed. The fact that the most popular reforms are defective does not lead us to the conclusion that no reforms are required! The next chapter proposes real solutions to real problems.

CHAPTER 10

REAL PROBLEMS, REAL SOLUTIONS

This final chapter addresses real problems of Canadian universities and proposes real solutions to them. The main ingredients of our recipe for university reform should surprise no one who has read the preceding chapters. We stress the importance of teaching and reflective inquiry, as well as the connection between them, the need to de-emphasize "cutting edge" research and page-counting publication, improvements to the performance of the federal research granting councils, new emphases in graduate education, and a more carefully considered role for sessional lecturers. We attempt to avoid the excesses of both an idealism so unbending that it amounts to utopianism and a realism so abject that it simply endorses the status quo. Readers may reach their own conclusions about our success (or lack of it), especially by judging the final section of this chapter, "Unclear Futures," in which we consider whether Canadian universities can indeed become genuine places to learn.

THE CENTRAL PROBLEM: NO PLACE TO LEARN

This book keeps returning to the central problem with Canadian universities, especially but not only the research-intensive universities. This central problem is that it is exceedingly difficult for an undergraduate student to acquire a first-rate higher education. It would not be misleading to say that this is *the* problem of Canadian universities. It would not be misleading but it would not be very enlightening either because the central problem really comprises several contributing problems. The central problem can be solved only by solving the contributing problems. In the course of this book we have identified many contributing problems. In this final chapter, in the interests of brevity and emphasis, we discuss only the most important problems and solutions.

TOO LITTLE TIME TO TEACH

A common misconception about university professors is that they don't work very hard. Most people think that the jobs of professors, like those of elementary and high school teachers, last only as long as the academic year. Since the university academic year is shorter by more than two months than that of the elementary and secondary school, it looks as though professors have a pretty soft job. When people discover that professors spend about the same amount of time in the classroom in a week as high school teachers spend each day, they are even more likely to think that professors have it made: short hours, long vacations, and good pay.

The truth is that, with few exceptions, professors work very hard. Unlike elementary and secondary teachers, they have twelve-month contracts. They are full-year employees of their university, with allowance for a contractually specified vacation, usually four weeks per year. Few professors take their full vacation, however. Moreover, few work less than a fifty-hour week. How, then, can they have too little time to teach? The answer, of course, is that most of their time is consumed by research intended to produce publications. Here we have a simple and straightforward problem: professors spend too much time on frontier research and too little on teaching. To this problem there is an equally simple and straightforward solution: they should spend more time on teaching and less on research. But this is, of course, a pseudo-solution. It is mere preaching, and preaching is not an effective way of motivating change, however gratifying it may be to the preacher and those already converted. We must address the *underlying* problems that cause the problem of too much research and too little teaching.

Mutual Enrichment Dogma

Readers will recall that mutual enrichment dogma asserts an inseparable connection between good teaching and good research. Good research stimulates good teaching and good teaching stimulates good research. Since most professors prefer research to teaching, this turns into the dogma that all good researchers are good teachers (but never the reverse). This encourages professors to devote the bulk of their time to research, stinting on teaching. This is clearly a problem underlying the problem that professors devote too much time to research and too little to teaching.

The solution is to reveal that the dogma is just that: a dogma. No systematic evidence supports it. Indeed, such evidence as exists suggests that there is a slight inverse correlation between good teaching and good research. Common sense yields the same conclusion. There are only so many hours in the day. Hours spent on frontier research are hours not spent on teaching or preparation for teaching, including reflective inquiry. Moreover, the fact that so many professors seek relief from teaching in order to devote more time to research indicates that *they* do not buy the mutual reinforcement dogma.

Since mutual reinforcement dogma is at best dubious, and most likely false, no university policy should rest on the pretence that it is true. In particular, in relation to basic career decisions (tenure, salary increments, promotion), no benefit of the doubt should be given to professors with weak teaching records who are productive researchers.

Quantity versus Quality in Research

Another reason why professors have too little time to teach is that research is assessed mainly on the basis of its quantity rather than its quality. Remarkably, high praise for a modern professor is to call her productive. A small number of brilliant scientists and scholars can get away with publications that are few but excellent. However, the research of most professors is judged on its amount rather than its breadth, depth, or originality. This practice is encouraged by the federal research granting councils, which award grants to those who publish prolifically. Some scientists and engineers we interviewed told us that it is common practice (which they engage in themselves) to publish three or four limited and incomplete articles rather than one thorough article, with a view to impressing the councils' peer reviewers with the high output.

This emphasis on quantity in research is certainly a factor in restricting the time available for teaching. Here are two partial and quite realistic solutions we think would bring about a quick, significant change for the better.

Within universities, at crucial points in a professor's career (tenure, promotion), he or she should be permitted to submit only a very small number of publications as evidence of strength in research. This would encourage professors to try to produce a few gems instead of pounds of gravel. Universities would now be obliged to honour their commitment to the quality of research, not merely its quantity. They would have to ask hard questions about the contribution of professorial research to substantial questions. Ideally, universities would ask, Does the body of research under examination raise distinctively new issues, challenge conventional wisdom, or illuminate important questions? Under this system and by definition, ten tedious articles could not trump two really good ones. In fact, tedious articles should be considered a demerit not a sign of achievement.

The federal research granting councils should base grants on quality rather than quantity. The government is perfectly entitled to insist on this without interfering in academic freedom by deciding what quality *is* in the various academic fields.

VIOLATIONS OF CONTRACT

The employment contracts of Canadian professors state that their principal responsibilities are teaching and research. At a few universities teaching is officially ranked higher than research, but more commonly they are ranked equally. No large university treats them equally, however. The actual rankings manifest themselves in the decisions universities make about the career advancement of professors. In the interviews we conducted, no professor, dean, vice-president, or president at the larger universities said that teaching was ranked as high as research. Asked to estimate the relative weights of the two activities, most professors said 70 percent research, 30 percent teaching. Even in smaller, primarily undergraduate universities, several science professors said that research outweighed teaching.

We now discuss under the heading of "violations of contract" two abuses which, legally, may or may not fit the definition. If these abuses are not illegal, they should be. Both relate to the evaluation of professors. One concerns research, the other teaching.

The abuse that concerns research has to do with research grants. For many decades in medicine and the sciences, and for the past fifteen years increasingly in the humanities and social sciences, professors have been rewarded (in crucial career decisions about tenure, pay, and promotion) for receiving research grants, whether from the federal research granting councils or from private foundations or corporations. This practice is a violation of contract because professors' contracts of employment do not require that they be fundraisers. If the practice of rewarding professors for receiving grants is not illegal, it should be. First, as a matter of principle, research should be judged on the basis of its quality, not on the basis of who paid for it or how much was paid for it. Second, donors of research grants are tempted to support projects that promise to yield results in the short run. This is particularly evident with grants to social scientists, many of which are openly acknowledged to be "strategic grants," that is, grants designed to provide policy advice regarding pressing social problems.[1] It is most unwise for universities to have a blanket policy of providing an incentive for professors to do research that has a quick payoff and thereby a disincentive to undertake important research that has a long period of germination. Finally, the evaluation and advancement of professors on the basis of the financial value of research grants mocks all ideals about higher education as the disinterested pursuit of truth.

The abuse that concerns teaching has to do with a fascination with novelty. In recent years the evaluation of teaching has been seduced by faddishness. To some extent, this fascination with novelty applies to subject matter. A cutting-edge teacher ("cutting edge" in contemporary Canadian universities, as in our corporations, means really good) is one who gives a course that no one has given before, especially if the subject matter of the new course is also novel. Thus, creating a course on some aspect of contemporary popular culture (an afternoon television talk show or a rap group) is seen as intrinsically meritorious.[2] However, the supposed excellence of novelty applies more to the style of teaching than to what is taught. Apparently, excellent teachers are now innovative, which is to say that they teach with new techniques, ideally computer software. This type of evaluation of teaching is, or should be, a violation of contract. Nothing in professors' contracts requires them to be hip, nor should they. Unquestionably it is a defect in a teacher to be unwilling to consider innovations in technique and use new techniques that promise improvements. However, it is also a defect to fail to make appropriate use of old techniques. If Professor Cardinal uses old techniques well and Professor Desjarlais uses "innovative" techniques badly, clearly Cardinal is a better teacher than Desjarlais. Moreover, if Cardinal uses old techniques well and Desjarlais uses new ones well, there is no reason to give Desjarlais a higher ranking. If it is now legally permissible for universities to reach any other conclusion, the law should be changed.

GRADUATE EDUCATION

The finishing school for professors of tomorrow is the graduate department of a discipline. In the process of acquiring a PhD in her field, the doctoral candidate works closely with several professors and learns firsthand what being a professor is all about. What does she do in graduate school? First, for a year or two she takes advanced courses in the two or three fields of her discipline in which she specializes. A philosophy graduate student, for example, might take courses in theory of knowledge and philosophy of science. Typically, these courses are quite specialized. Second, after her course work and further independent study, she takes comprehensive examinations. These examinations, which usually have written and oral components, are not comprehensive in the sense that the candidate is required to know at least a bit about all parts of philosophy. They require only that she have a good grasp of her areas of specialization (in our example, theory of knowledge and philosophy of science). Third, having completed the comprehensive examinations, she writes her PhD dissertation. A PhD thesis in mathematics is a very different work from one in history. However, they have in common that they are supposed to make "an original contribution to knowledge." In order to be original, they have to be on a topic, or an aspect of a topic, that has never been studied closely before. Consequently, they tend to be highly specialized. The title of an imaginary philosophy thesis might be "Gregory Vlastos' Analysis of Plato's Theory of Recollection."

Two features of this education are particularly striking. The first is that it is remarkably narrow and specialized. This narrowness is ironic in light of today's calls for interdisciplinary and multidisciplinary studies. In fact, PhD candidates, far from being encouraged to explore other disciplines, are not even required to acquire substantial familiarity with their own. The imaginary philosophy student we considered above is not required to spend any time at all during her graduate studies on philosophy of religion or moral philosophy. The second striking feature of the PhD program is that it is all about research. Course work deals with conventional lore, recent thinking, and avant-garde speculation in the student's specialty. Comprehensive examinations test mastery of the specialty. The thesis requires painstaking research of a narrow topic. No part of the graduate school education involves preparation for life as a teacher.[3] With this kind of preparation, it is little wonder that so many professors enter their profession not only with a preference for research over teaching but also with a belief that research is far more important than teaching. This is certainly part of the problem. Is there a workable solution?

We propose three innovations in graduate education that are intended to increase the likelihood that professors-to-be have both the inclination and the ability to teach well. PhD students should be required to take two courses on teaching. One should be a how-to course. Coordinated by one of the best teachers in the various departments, with visits from excellent teachers from within the department and from other departments, this course should deal with both mechanical matters (how to write on a blackboard legibly, how to construct a useful course outline) and more intangible ones (how to encourage students who talk too little and how to discourage those who talk too much). Each student in the course should be required to do some student teaching. Their assignments would be carefully scrutinized by experienced professors. Feedback and evaluation would be continuous. Departments with major graduate programs would be expected to put substantial resources to the task.

The second course should deal with questions about the history, problems, and prospects of university education. In this course, students should study and discuss (for example) agreements and disagreements about the nature of higher education, issues about the proper role of professors in community service, and debates about current issues such as political correctness. It is important that students complete assignments and receive grades in these courses, just as in the disciplinary subject matter courses. Teaching is important, and this message should not be diluted by giving graduate students the impression that the courses on teaching are secondary. In addition, graduate students unwilling or unable to perform satisfactorily in the teaching courses would never receive doctoral degrees, and hence would never be unleashed on university students, to the benefit of everyone concerned.

To give reality to the pious hope that graduate students will stretch themselves beyond the confines of their own discipline, students should be required to have an outside minor. The requirement of an outside minor is common in the United States and is one of the best features of American graduate education. The requirement of an outside minor is that a PhD student must actually take graduate courses in a discipline other than her own. For example, the requirement in political science could be that, for every three courses she takes in her home department she must take one in another department. The outside minor for a political science graduate student could vary considerably with the student's interests. Whatever the minor might be, from forestry to anthropology, it would raise what is desirable in the call for interdisciplinary study from piety to practice.

Comprehensive examinations should be much broader than they are now. They should not concentrate exclusively on the student's special interests within her discipline. They should include questions about the outside minor subject and about teaching.

We do not call for a revolution in graduate education. Much that is done in PhD programs is very good. Nevertheless, there is a crying need for greater breadth and better preparation for teaching. Our proposals for reform address these needs directly with specific requirements rather than mere expressions of hope.

SESSIONAL LECTURERS AND PROFESSORS

Sessional lecturers, and therefore professors, are employed ineffectively. Sessionals, to use the common designation, are either working on their PhD theses or have recently completed them. Unavoidably, these theses are quite narrow and specialized. Invariably, however, sessional lecturers are assigned to teach demanding first- and second-year courses in which the emphasis is on generality rather than specialization. In other words, sessional lecturers are required to teach the courses that they are least well equipped to teach. Moreover, the courses they are required to teach are the very ones that professors are (or should be) well prepared to teach.

As professors gain more and more experience and maturity, they should be better and better able to teach the junior courses that require some years of reflective inquiry. With each passing year they should become better able to lay out the basic principles of their subject, explain how these principles manifest themselves in various branches of the subject, understand broadly the relationship between their subject and others, become better equipped with examples and adept at using them, and grasp more fully both the agreements and disagreements among practitioners of their subject in order to answer tough questions from students. In brief, professors should teach the more demanding, more general courses. Sessional lecturers should teach the more specialized courses.

There is a major problem here, since prevailing practice is exactly the opposite of what it should be. However, this makes the solution all the more obvious. That is, simply reverse prevailing practice. Sessional lecturers should teach only more advanced, more specialized courses, and junior courses should be taught only by tenured professors. Two additional points should be made about this recommendation. First, although we say that only professors should teach junior courses, we do not say that professors should not teach advanced courses. That would be preposterous for several reasons, not the least of them being that professors are responsible for the teaching and supervision of PhD students.[4] Second, our distinction between junior courses and more advanced, more specialized courses is in no way a qualification of the view, stated emphatically in Chapter 4, the chapter on teaching, that courses that simply advance a professor's narrow research interests are entirely unacceptable. The elimination of all such courses is one of our strongest recommendations.

TEACHING RESPONSIBILITIES

Our recommendations entail that professors devote a larger proportion of their time to teaching. (The exception to this generalization is the small, primarily undergraduate institutions like Acadia, Trent, and Lethbridge where, for the most part, professors devote enough time and effort to undergraduate teaching.) Three of our recommendations, in particular, dictate this change in priorities. The first of these is the recommendation that junior courses should be taught by professors rather than by sessional lecturers, and the second is that there should be no huge introductory courses. Since there now are huge introductory courses, and since many junior courses are now taught by sessionals, the changes we propose obviously require professors to spend more time in the classroom. In addition, we propose that graduate education should be altered so as to place far more emphasis on preparing doctoral students for the teaching component of their future careers as professors. The adoption of this proposal would require professors to do more teaching both inside and outside the classroom.

Although these proposals require more teaching, they do not threaten to turn Canadian universities into pedagogical sweatshops. First, the implementation of our recommendations would relieve professors of the burden of producing a steady stream of research publications. Second, the serious teaching we propose involves a great deal of the reflective inquiry that should be given a much heavier weighting within the research contributions of professors. Finally, we recognize – or, rather, emphasize – that the supervision of graduate students is a very important dimension of teaching.

PUBLIC RESEARCH

Chapter 8 notes how universities, firms, and governments now establish research consortia, "partnerships" in the vernacular, whose aim is to develop and bring to market commercially viable products and processes. An unacceptable aspect of partnerships and increased applied research is greater secrecy in university research. University researchers now sometimes sign agreements with research funders that allow for either the delay of publication of findings or the censorship of draft publications.

Such practices should be banned by interuniversity agreement. That is, no professor or researcher associated with a Canadian university nor any research centre or department of a Canadian university should be permitted to engage in agreements that delay or censor publications. Such a prohibition is entirely justified because all universities claim dedication to free research and open debate. In banning unnecessary restraints on research and publication, they are simply living up to one of their basic claims. Agreements that allow for publication delays and censorship are not justified by any principles of higher education. To the contrary, they are justified by the commercial drives of research funders, by the need for research funds in universities, and by political arguments about the need for universities to be relevant. These are arguments about money, influence, and public relations not about education.

Universities compete against each other for prestige, public visibility, and research preeminence. For this reason, an interuniversity agreement is required. Otherwise, companies will avoid universities with demanding rules about open research and go to ones with lax rules and practices. Moreover, if research consortia are indeed essential to Canada's economic well-being, they should be little deterred by greater obligations for transparency and openness in the communication of research results.

PUBLIC SPACE FOR STUDENTS

Our basic theme is that Canadian universities are defective as places to learn because most professors are preoccupied with research and regard teaching as a necessary evil. However, our emphasis on this central theme may leave the impression that we believe that all teaching and all learning at universities takes place in classrooms or other formal sites. Of course this is incorrect. Some teaching of students by professors takes place in informal settings: coffee shops, pubs, and common rooms. More frequently, and more importantly, students learn from each other. Such learning is a major part of a good university education. A reliable sign of a good course is that groups of students in it meet together to discuss it. And one of the most reliable signs that a university is a good one is that students spend a good deal of time conversing with each other about a wide range of subjects.

Students cannot engage in these important conversations unless they have places to do so. During the past two decades such spaces have been eliminated from Canadian university campuses at an alarming rate. Nowadays it is often impossible for a group of students to find a place on campus to chat other than a large, noisy cafeteria or pub. Canadian universities could make an easy first step by refusing to eliminate any more public space for students. Then they should shift priorities away from claims on space for researchers to claims on space for students and undergraduate teaching. Finally, the next round of complaint about the deterioration of university infrastructure should stress the need to replace lost student space.

UNCLEAR FUTURES

The reforms proposed here are quite idealistic in that they call for signifi-cant changes of opinions, attitudes, and conduct, especially on the part of professors. Are they also tolerably realistic in the sense that the people in a position to implement them could do so if they chose to? Pretty clearly they are realistic in this sense. We do not call for the transformation of uni-versities into institutions that bear no resemblance to existing ones. We do not call for professors or students to take up activities that are radically at variance with university traditions. We do not propose patterns of conduct that are morally dubious. Our reforms do not entail huge new financial burdens. If the proper test of the practicality of our proposals is that what we say should be done could be done, we pass that test.

There is, however, another test of practicality. This test is not whether the implementation of the reforms we propose is possible but whether it is probable. Is there any likelihood that the reforms proposed here will be implemented? A fair answer to this question requires that we consider not just the near future but also the more distant future. Canada is not a land marked by dramatic, rapid changes in its institutions, and universities are conservative institutions even by Canadian standards.

The Near Future

Is there any real prospect that Canadian universities will move in the direc-tion we recommend in the near future? As we noted in Chapter 1, we believe that Canadian universities enjoy a good deal of autonomy. To a considerable extent, they can act as they wish, regardless of the preferences of, for example, provincial governments, corporations, and professional associations.[5] This view directs us to look, in the first place, at the array of forces within universities.

As we have observed repeatedly, the professoriate strongly supports the status quo. Outside the small, primarily undergraduate universities like Acadia, Trent, and Brandon, no more than one Canadian professor in ten would support most of the reforms we propose. Moreover, few of the reformers would be under the age of fifty. University administrators would come even closer to a unanimous conservatism. It is difficult to estimate the array of opinions among students because their views about higher education are seldom systematically examined. However, it is safe to say that both those who would favour and those who would oppose our proposals are small minorities. Far more important is the fact that most students have given practically no thought to alternatives to universities as they are currently constituted. Students are not a potent force one way or the other. Within the university there is thus limited support for our reforms. We find no reason to believe that the level of support will rise in the near future.

Consider now pressures for reform originating from outside universities. The only plausible outside candidates for pressing universities to reform themselves are governments, parents of current students, and parents of university-bound students currently in high school. Governments, federal and provincial, seldom challenge basic university priorities. As long as universities live, relatively quietly, within their budgets, governments are happy to live and let live. Moreover, in the 1990s and into the third millennium, universities and the Government of Canada have worked harmoniously to strengthen research on Canadian campuses. Many parents of current and prospective students would prefer lower fees and a more manageable student-loan policy. However, few of them understand universities well enough to understand how to push for substantial changes in them, even supposing that many of them wish to do so, which is doubtful. Moreover, most parents are inhibited from challenging the practices and priorities of universities by their belief that professors, and deans and presidents even more, are almost unbelievably intelligent and well informed.

In summary, within universities there is at present no significant support for the reforms we propose. Furthermore, no politically weighty calls for reform emanate from outside. This array of forces will not change in the near future.

The More Distant Future

It is usually easy to predict the near future, especially the near future of conservative institutions like Canadian universities. The safe prediction is that tomorrow will be pretty much like today. However, when we try to foresee the more distant future we enter a much hazier area – one in which predictions are at best informed conjectures. Moreover, the near future, in which we can speak sensibly of predictions rather than conjectures, is often remarkably short-lived. How many people predicted, even two years before their occurrence, the collapse of the Soviet regime, the AIDS epidemic, or the plague of cellular phones? Closer to home, who foresaw the rapid rise of a separatist party in Quebec, the emergence of Toronto as one of the world's most culturally diverse cities, or the mushrooming of women's competitive team sports? Specifically in regard to Canadian universities, who would have guessed in 1950 that in 1970 religion would have practically disappeared as a major preoccupation of most students and professors? Who would have guessed in 1970 that in 1990 the majority of undergraduate students would be women? Who would have guessed in 1980 that in 2000 computer science would be regarded by most students as infinitely more interesting and important than history?

As we discussed in Chapter 2, the story of Canadian universities is in part a story of major changes. One thing about the more distant future we can predict with confidence, and not merely surmise, is that there will be further important changes in the future. Is it reasonable to conjecture that the reforms we propose may be in the future of Canadian universities? We think it is.

Once again, our perspective directs us to look at the array of forces both inside and outside universities, paying particular attention to the former. However, let us begin with the outside forces, since we have little to say about them. Our view about the outside forces is that, in the more distant future as now, their influence on the shape of universities will be comparatively minor. However, we note two changes that could be somewhat important. The first is that there is much to be said for, and little against, the federal research granting councils shifting from research productivity to research quality in the awarding of grants, with no significant political fall-out from making the change. So it may actually occur. This change in itself would have an immediate and highly desirable effect on the assessment of research within universities. The second is that, as the children of the baby boomers make their way through university, both the number and the proportion of Canadian citizens with exposure to university life will rise significantly. This fact by no means guarantees that public attitudes toward universities will change. However, it does ensure the presence of a larger constituency of citizens somewhat familiar with the workings of universities and hence less likely to overestimate the wisdom and public-spiritedness of professors and administrators. Slowly but surely, universities may be demystified.

Consider now the array of forces within universities. In the deeply conservative early years of the twenty-first century, it is easy to assume that no one cares about meaningful change. But this view is clearly wrong. For example, university feminists are very serious about significant change and some of them work hard at it. We do not suggest for a moment that they support the reforms we propose. Aside from their concern with changes in curriculum, they are thoroughgoing conservatives with respect to the structure and functioning of universities. Their main concern is equity within existing structures and practices. We mention them for two reasons. The first is to point out that there are serious reformers in universities even in conservative times. The second is to suggest that in the more distant future feminists – perhaps the next generation of them – might be strong proponents of our reforms. It is far from inconceivable that feminists will come to believe that deeper thinking and more committed teaching are more important than increasing the number of female professors and senior administrators.

Second, the prospects for reform in the more distant future may be greatest in the institutions labelled by *Maclean's* magazine as comprehensive universities. Comprehensive universities are larger and more diverse than the small, primarily undergraduate institutions like Mount Allison and Brock. They have some professional programs and they place considerable emphasis on research – some of them, like York and Carleton, have major doctoral programs in some subjects. But they differ from the universities labelled by *Maclean's* as medical/doctoral in that they lack medical schools. This difference, which might seem to be a minor difference of degree, is profound in practice. Professors of medicine are the supermodels of academia. They have more prestige than computer scientists and higher pay than marketing experts. They teach less than physicists and receive far more and larger grants than engineers. They are at the pinnacle of the modern academic pyramid. No matter what they do, the comprehensive universities can never match the dazzle of research universities with medical schools that conduct sophisticated research. They may well decide that it would be better to be first-rate under new rules than also-rans under the old ones. The best hope for reform may be universities like New Brunswick, Waterloo, and Victoria.

Third, it is virtually a commonplace among thoughtful commentators at the prestigious private American universities that undergraduate education is a mess needing to be repaired.[6] Ironically, many prominent Canadian professors and administrators who deeply admire major American universities may be forced by their own loyalties to take seriously the need for far-reaching changes.

Finally, the preceding point is somewhat unfair. It suggests that most influential people in Canadian universities are motivated by a desire to emulate those they admire. There is a lot of that going around. But it is wrong to suggest that Canadian university leaders are contemptuous of evidence and argument. Most of them will weigh the evidence and arguments put forward by their American colleagues. To the extent that they do so, we believe they will be drawn to the kind of critical analysis and proposals for reform presented in this book. Although the shape of Canadian universities in the more distant future is unclear, it is not preposterous to hope, as well as to urge, that they become genuine places to learn.

NOTES

Chapter 1: No Place to Learn

1 "The Knowledge Factory: A Survey of Universities," *The Economist,* 4 October 1997, 4.

2 Clark Kerr, *The Uses of the University,* 3rd ed. (Cambridge, MA: Harvard University Press, 1982).

3 Christopher Jencks and David Riesman, *The Academic Revolution* (Garden City, NY: Doubleday, 1968), 221.

4 For an overview of the research university in the United States see Jonathan R. Cole, Elinor G. Barber, and Stephen R. Graubard, eds., *The Research University in a Time of Discontent* (Baltimore and London: Johns Hopkins University Press, 1994).

5 Boyer Commission on Educating Undergraduates in the Research University, *Reinventing Undergraduate Education: A Blueprint for America's Research Universities* (Princeton, NJ: Carnegie Foundation for the Advancement of Teaching, 1997), 4.

6 For an impressive articulation of this theme see Eric A. Nordlinger, *On the Autonomy of the Democratic State* (Cambridge, MA: Harvard University Press, 1981).

7 Our interviews were conducted by a loose methodology. Our sample of universities and professors were nonrandom. We interviewed colleagues who were recommended by others, who taught in different disciplines, who were willing to meet with us, and who had different viewpoints. Interviews ranged in length from half an hour to two hours. Travel for the interviews was made possible by a grant from the vice-president (Research) at the University of Alberta.

8 Commission of Inquiry on Canadian University Education, *Report,* (Ottawa: Association of Universities and Colleges of Canada, 1991).

Chapter 2: The Canadian University

1 Readers wanting further information on the development of higher education in Canada should consult David M. Cameron, *More Than an Academic Question: Universities, Government, and Public Policy in Canada* (Halifax: Institute for Research on Public Policy, 1991); Glen A. Jones, ed., *Higher Education in Canada: Different Systems, Different Perspectives* (New York: Garland Publishing, 1997); and A.B. McKillop, *Matters of Mind: The University in Ontario, 1791-1951* (Toronto: University of Toronto Press, 1994). And for a detailed account of the development of a Canadian university see P.B. Waite, *The Lives of Dalhousie University,* vols. 1 and 2 (Montreal and Kingston: McGill–Queen's University Press, 1994 and 1998).

2 Louis-Philippe Bonneau and J.A. Corry, *Quest for the Optimum: Research Policy in the Universities of Canada,* vol. 1 (Ottawa: Association of Universities and Colleges of Canada, 1972), 17.

3 Robert P. Wolff, *The Ideal of the University* (Boston: Beacon Press, 1969).

4 P.B. Waite, *The Lives of Dalhousie University,* vol. 1 (Montreal and Kingston: McGill–Queen's University Press, 1994), 118-20.

5 Clark Kerr, *The Uses of the University,* 3rd ed. (Cambridge, MA: Harvard University Press, 1982), 47.

6 George Dennis O'Brien, *All the Essential Half-Truths about Higher Education* (Chicago: University of Chicago Press, 1998), 21.

7 For details see McKillop, *Matters of Mind,* especially chapters 3 and 13.

8 Abraham Flexner, *Universities: American, English, German* (New Brunswick, NJ: Transaction Publishers, 1994), 85.

9 McKillop, *Matters of Mind,* 78.

10 Christopher Jencks and David Riesman, *The Academic Revolution* (Garden City, NY: Doubleday, 1968), chapter 5.

11 Organized religions remained actively concerned about the content of university teaching, the religious affiliations of professors, and the religious implications of university research well into the 1960s. For details see Michiel Horn, *Academic Freedom in Canada: A History* (Toronto: University of Toronto Press, 1999), chapter 10.

12 "The Knowledge Factory: A Survey of Universities," *The Economist,* 4 October 1997, 12.

13 This is the strongly asserted claim of a well-known critique of Canadian universities. See David J. Bercuson, Robert Bothwell, and J.L. Granatstein, *Petrified Campus: The Crisis in Canada's Universities* (Toronto: Random House, 1997). We disagree deeply with this view and even more strongly with the authors' uncritical admiration of research by "superstar" professors.

14 J.A. Corry, *Farewell the Ivory Tower: Universities in Transition* (Montreal and London: McGill–Queen's University Press, 1970), 101-12.

Chapter 3: Universities in Action

1 For details see Tom Pocklington, "The Place of Political Science in Canadian Universities," *Canadian Journal of Political Science* 31, 4 (1998), especially 656-7.

2 Note that if the convictions in question are that deep, they will be shared by most faculty members in other faculties in the dean's university, by most members of the faculties of other universities in Canada, and ultimately by the supreme arbiters: professors in major American universities. Moreover, if the opinions are that deeply and widely shared, the dean will almost certainly be part of the consensus: people who march to their own drummers are not likely candidates for administrative positions in universities. So the examples that follow are a bit far-fetched.

Chapter 4: University Teaching

1 Louis-Philippe Bonneau and J.A. Corry, *Quest for the Optimum: Research Policy in the Universities of Canada* (Ottawa: Association of Universities and Colleges of Canada, 1972), 20.

2 There is another group of exceptional students whom we are not sure how to classify. These are students who, as they mature, are concerned mainly with exhibiting their skills, imagination, or even virtuosity. We have in mind especially most students in the fine arts (art, music, and drama) and some in mathematics and computing studies.

3 This time is for colleagues as well as for students who may drop by.

4 We have nothing interesting to say about great teachers, except that their proportion of the teaching force does not seem to fluctuate much. A study of great teachers would be a wonderfully worthwhile piece of frontier research and reflective inquiry.

5 Inevitably, even the most talented, committed, and enthusiastic teachers sometimes perform badly. It is a reasonable conjecture that professors who regard teaching as preeminent are more upset by these poor performances than are those who see teaching as a price to be paid for research opportunities.

6 Sid Gilbert, "Quality Education: Does Class Size Matter?" *Research File* 1, 1 (April 1995). Readers may draw what conclusions they wish from the fact that this essay was first published in *University Affairs* by the Association of Universities and Colleges of Canada, which is the organ of university and college administrators, and that it is still featured on their web site as the first of their research reports. Gilbert's essay can be found at <www.aucc.ca/en/statbody.html> (accessed 17 December 2001).

7 No author, *Maclean's,* 9 November 1992, 39.

8 The average grade at Harvard is reportedly now B+. Bear in mind that this average is not based only on the grades of the brilliant scholarship students from Oklahoma and Idaho but also on those of the children of alumni.

9 For details see Murray Sperber, *Beer and Circus: How Big Time College Sports Is Crippling Undergraduate Education* (New York: Henry Holt, 2000), especially chapter 10.

Chapter 5: Research and Reflective Inquiry

1 J.A. Corry, *Farewell the Ivory Tower: Universities in Transition* (Montreal and London: McGill-Queen's University Press, 1970), 89.

2 Abraham Flexner, *Universities: American, English, German* (New Brunswick, NJ: Transaction Publishers, 1994).

3 Corry, *Farewell* and J.A. Corry, *My Life and Work, A Happy Partnership: Memoirs of J.A. Corry* (Kingston, ON: Queen's University Press, 1981).

4 For a flavour of the American debate see Martin Anderson, *Impostors in the Temple* (New York: Simon and Schuster, 1992); Jacques Barzun, *The American University: How It Runs, Where It Is Going,* 2nd ed. (Chicago: University of Chicago Press, 1993); Benjamin R. Barber, *An Aristocracy of Everyone: The Politics of Education and the Future of America* (New York: Ballantine Books, 1992); Allan Bloom, *The Closing of the American Mind* (New York: Simon and Schuster, 1987); Ernest L. Boyer, *Scholarship Reconsidered: Priorities for the Professoriate* (New York: Carnegie Foundation for the Advancement of Teaching, 1990); Jonathan R. Cole, Elinor G. Barber, and Stephen R. Graubard, eds., *The Research University in a Time of Discontent* (Baltimore and London: Johns Hopkins University Press, 1994); Donald Kennedy, *Academic Duty* (Cambridge, MA: Harvard University Press, 1997); Roger Kimball, *Tenured Radicals: How Politics Has Corrupted Higher Education* (New York: Harper and Row, 1990); George Dennis O'Brien, *All the Essential Half-Truths about Higher Education* (Chicago: University of Chicago Press, 1998); J.L. Pelikan, *The Idea of the University: A Reexamination* (New Haven, CT: Yale University Press, 1992); Robert Solomon and Jon Solomon, *Up the University: Recreating Higher Education in America* (New York: Addison and Wesley, 1993); Page Smith, *Killing the Spirit: Higher Education in America* (New York: Viking Penguin, 1990); Charles J. Sykes, *Profscam: Professors and the Demise of Higher Education* (Washington, DC: Regnery Gateway, 1988); and Robert P. Wolff, *The Ideal of the University* (Boston: Beacon Press, 1969).

5 Boyer Commission on Educating Undergraduates in the Research University, *Reinventing Undergraduate Education: A Blueprint for America's Research Universities* (Princeton, NJ: Carnegie Foundation for the Advancement of Teaching, 1997), 18.

6 Charles O. Anderson, *Prescribing the Life of the Mind* (Madison: University of Wisconsin Press, 1993), 7.

7 Brock University, *Submission to the Commission of Inquiry on Canadian University Education,* 1990.

8 Murray Ross, *The Way Must Be Tried: Memoirs of a University Man* (Toronto: Stoddart, 1992).

9 Interviews, University of Northern British Columbia, June 1996.

10 The following sources provide an overview: Bloom, *The Closing of the American Mind*; David Bromwich, *Politics By Other Means: Higher Education and Group Thinking* (New Haven, CT: Yale University Press, 1992); Peter C. Emberley, *Zero Tolerance:*

Hot Button Politics in Canada's Universities (Toronto: Penguin Books, 1996); Michiel Horn, *Academic Freedom in Canada: A History* (Toronto: University of Toronto Press, 1999); Jay A. Labinger, "The Science Wars and the American Academic Profession," *Daedalus* 126, 4 (1997): 201-20; John R. Searle, "Rationality and Realism, What Is at Stake?" in *The Research University in a Time of Discontent,* ed. Cole, Barber, and Graubard, 55-84.

11 Boyer Commission, *Reinventing Undergraduate Education,* 4.

12 Christopher Jencks and David Riesman, *The Academic Revolution* (Garden City, NY: Doubleday, 1968).

13 Robert M. Hutchins, *The Higher Learning in America* (New Haven, CT: Yale University Press, 1936), 3.

14 Kennedy, *Academic Duty,* 7.

15 Interviews were undertaken at the University of Alberta, Carleton University, the University of Northern British Columbia, Dalhousie University, the Technical University of Nova Scotia (now called Dal Tech), and Mount Saint Vincent University. Nonrandom samples of universities and professors were selected. For details see Chapter 1, n. 7.

16 Barzun, *The American University,* 231.

17 Clark Kerr, *The Uses of the University,* 3rd ed. (Cambridge, MA: Harvard University Press, 1982), 51-5.

18 Louis-Philippe Bonneau and J.A. Corry, *Quest for the Optimum: Research Policy in the Universities of Canada* (Ottawa, ON: Association of Universities and Colleges of Canada, 1972), especially 30-1.

19 Hutchins, *Higher Learning in America,* 23.

20 Anderson, *Prescribing the Life of the Mind,* 72.

21 Bonneau and Corry, *Quest for the Optimum.* Semantics arise at this point. Corry and Bonneau make a clear distinction between reflective inquiry and scholarship. Scholarship, in their view, involves a rich and detailed account of a discrete phenomenon. A problem arises in that the term "scholarship" is widely used by others to describe what Corry and Bonneau call reflective inquiry. Ernest L. Boyer's well-known work *Scholarship Reconsidered* makes an argument similar to that of Corry and Bonneau. He decries universities' contemporary obsession with narrowly defined research. He argues for a sweeping view of professorial obligation that embraces scholarship in several dimensions, including the scholarship of teaching and the scholarship of synthesis. Corry and Bonneau's idea of reflective inquiry embraces Boyer's various dimensions of scholarship.

22 Bonneau and Corry, *Quest for the Optimum,* 31.

23 One exception to this is the University of Alberta's public celebration of the scholarship of textbook writing in 1996.

24 Barzun, *The American University,* 222.

25 Jencks and Riesman, *The Academic Revolution,* chapters 4 and 12.

26 Bonneau and Corry, *Quest for the Optimum,* 29.

27 Barzun, *The American University,* 20-1.

28 Smith, *Killing the Spirit,* 7.

29 For overviews see Kennedy, *Academic Duty*; John W. Langford, "Secrecy, Partnership and the Ownership of Knowledge in the University," *Intellectual Property Journal* 6 (June 1991): 155-69; Albert S. Meyerhoff, "Science and the Public Trust: The Need for Reform" in *Universities in Crisis: A Medieval Institution in the Twenty-First Century,* ed. William A. Neilson and Chad Gaffield, 69-86 (Montreal: Institute for Research on Public Policy, 1986); and Sheila Slaughter and Larry L. Leslie, *Academic Capitalism: Politics, Policies and the Entrepreneurial University* (Baltimore and London: Johns Hopkins University Press, 1997).

30 Kennedy, *Academic Duty.*

31 Hutchins, *Higher Learning in America.*

Chapter 6: Teaching and Research at Canadian Universities

1 Joseph Ben-David, "Research and Teaching in the Universities," in *The Western University on Trial,* ed. John W. Chapman (Berkeley: University of California Press, 1983), 91.

2 Royal Society of Canada, *Realizing the Potential: A Strategy for University Research in Canada* (Ottawa: Royal Society of Canada, 1991).

3 Ibid., 9.

4 Ibid., 1.

5 Commission of Inquiry on Canadian University Education, *Report* (Ottawa: Association of Universities and Colleges of Canada, 1991).

6 Ibid., 13.

7 Ibid., 31.

8 Kenneth J. Feldman, "Research, Productivity and Scholarly Accomplishment of College Teachers as Related to their Instructional Effectiveness: A Review and Exploration," *Research in Higher Education* 26, 3 (1987): 227-98.

9 Larry Milligan, "Basic Findings from the Research Literature," Workshop 6: The Linkages between Teaching and Research, Association of Universities and Colleges of Canada Symposium, Winnipeg, November 1993, 3.

10 Christopher Jencks and David Riesman, *The Academic Revolution* (Garden City, NY: Doubleday, 1968), chapters 1, 4, 6, and 12.

11 Henry Rosovsky, *The University: An Owner's Manual* (New York and London: W.W. Norton, 1990), especially chapter 5.

12 Ibid., 90.

13 Ibid.

14 J.L. Pelikan, *The Idea of the University: A Reexamination* (New Haven, CT: Yale University Press, 1992), 123.

15 Rosovsky admits that research-driven professors are inferior on these key points. Speaking of "professorial teachers" he remarks: "Many achieve great skill in using the Socratic method – skillful and creative class guidance. They tend to read the essays of their students with great attention and many are famous for the length and thoroughness of their comments." Rosovsky, *The University*, 93.

16 Louis-Philippe Bonneau and J.A. Corry, *Quest for the Optimum: Research Policy in the Universities of Canada* (Ottawa: Association of Universities and Colleges of Canada, 1972), 50-1.

17 Peter C. Emberley, *Zero Tolerance: Hot Button Politics in Canada's Universities* (Toronto: Penguin Books, 1996), especially 79-86.

18 Ibid., 85.

19 Michiel Horn, *Academic Freedom in Canada: A History* (Toronto: University of Toronto Press, 1999), 345-6.

20 David J. Bercuson, Robert Bothwell, and J.L. Granatstein, *Petrified Campus: The Crisis in Canada's Universities* (Toronto: Random House 1997), 65.

21 Horn, *Academic Freedom*, 346.

22 A good example of this tendency is George Dennis O'Brien, *All the Essential Half-Truths about Higher Education* (Chicago: University of Chicago Press, 1998), especially chapter 4.

23 Donald Kennedy, *Academic Duty* (Cambridge, MA: Harvard University Press, 1997), 25.

Chapter 7: Ethics in Canadian Universities

1 The account in this and succeeding paragraphs is based mainly on two documents: H.W. Arthurs, Roger A. Blais, and Jon Thompson, *Integrity in Scholarship: A Report to Concordia University* (Montreal: Concordia University, April 1994); and John Scott Cowan, *Lessons from the Fabrikant File: A Report to the Board of Governors of Concordia University* (Montreal: Concordia University, May 1994). These documents are commonly known as the Arthurs Report and the Cowan Report, respectively, and are hereafter cited as such. Although it is less germane to our inquiry, we also consulted Philip C. Levi, *Concordia University Special Audit Report on Specific Accounts of the Faculty of Engineering and Computer Science* (Montreal: Concordia University, July 1994).

2 All three of these men held positions of authority in relation to Fabrikant. T.S. Sankar was chair of the Department of Mechanical Engineering. M.N.S. Swamy was dean of the Faculty of Engineering and Computer Science. And S. Sankar was the director of CONCAVE.

3 These studies are cited in full in footnote 1 above.

4 Cowan Report, 10.

5 Ibid., 5. Corresponding to this assessment, Cowan's first recommendation is that all academics offered administrative positions should be encouraged, and in some cases required, to take some management training.

6 Some universities, especially the big ones, have vice-presidents who lack academic
  credentials. They are in charge of matters such as buildings and grounds, finances,
  and nonacademic personnel.
7 Arthurs Report, 3.
8 Ibid., 3-4.
9 Ibid., 8-9.

Chapter 8: Universities in Business
1 For a useful overview see A.B. McKillop, *Matters of Mind: The University in Ontario,
  1791-1951* (Toronto: University of Toronto Press, 1994).
2 John Ralston Saul, *The Unconscious Civilization* (Toronto: House of Anansi Press,
  1995).
3 James Engell and Anthony Dangerfield as cited in Eyal Press and Jennifer Washburn,
  "The Kept University," *The Atlantic Monthly* (March 2000): 52.
4 Robert Hutchins, the iconoclastic president of the University of Chicago, made this
  point in 1936. See Robert M. Hutchins, *The Higher Learning in America* (New Haven,
  CT: Yale University Press, 1936).
5 A substantial literature describes, analyzes, and evaluates new public management. A
  valuable guide is Peter Aucoin, *The New Public Management: Canada in Comparative
  Perspective* (Montreal: Institute for Research on Public Policy, 1995). See also Henry
  Mintzberg, "Managing Government, Governing Management," *Harvard Business
  Review,* May-June 1996, 75-83.
6 Charles O. Anderson, *Prescribing the Life of the Mind* (Madison: University of Wisconsin Press, 1993).
7 Sheila Slaughter, *The Higher Learning and High Technology: Dynamics of Higher Education Policy Formation* (Albany: State University of New York Press, 1990), 180.
8 Ibid., 29. For other overviews see John W. Langford, "Secrecy, Partnership and the
  Ownership of Knowledge in the University," *Intellectual Property Journal* 6 (June
  1991): 155-69; Janice Newsome and Howard Buchbinder, *The University Means Business* (Toronto: Garamond Press, 1988), Roger G. Noll, ed., *Challenges to Research Universities* (Washington, DC: Brookings Institution, 1998); Eyal Press and Jennifer
  Washburn, "The Kept University," *The Atlantic Monthly* (March 2000): 39-54; Sheila
  Slaughter and Larry L. Leslie, *Academic Capitalism: Politics, Policies and the Entrepre-
  neurial University* (Baltimore and London: Johns Hopkins University Press, 1997);
  Neil Tudiver, *Universities for Sale: Resisting Corporate Control over Canadian Higher
  Education* (Toronto: James Lorimer, 1999); and James L. Turk, ed., *The Corporate
  Campus: Commercialization and the Dangers to Canada's Colleges and Universities*
  (Toronto: James Lorimer, 2000). A laudatory analysis of universities' role in the
  knowledge economy is Heather Munroe-Blum with James Duderstadt and Sir
  Graeme Davies, *Growing Ontario's Innovation System: The Strategic Role of University*

Research, report prepared for the Government of Ontario (Toronto, 1999). Munroe-Blum's report is noteworthy for its uncritical analysis of universities' roles in the knowledge economy. Her view is that universities are integral to the economic prospects of Canada and Ontario.

9 "The Knowledge Factory: A Survey of Universities," *The Economist,* 4 October 1997, 1-22.

10 For an excellent discussion see Newsome and Buchbinder, *The University Means Business.*

11 Wesley M. Cohen, Richard Florida, Lucien Randazzese, and John Walsh, "Industry and the Academy: Uneasy Partners in the Cause of Technological Advance," in *Challenges to Research Universities,* ed. Roger G. Noll (Washington, DC: Brookings Institution, 1998), 171-200.

12 Ibid., 78-9.

13 For an excellent overview see Daniel J. Kevles, "A Time for Audacity: What the Past Has to Teach the Present about Science and the Federal Government," in *Universities and Their Leadership,* ed. William G. Bowen and Harold T. Shapiro (Princeton, NJ: Princeton University Press, 1998), 199-240.

14 Clark Kerr, *The Uses of the University,* 3rd ed. (Cambridge, MA: Harvard University Press, 1982).

15 Maxine Singer, "On the Future of America's Scientific Enterprise," in *Universities and Their Leadership,* ed. William G. Bowen and Harold T. Shapiro (Princeton, NJ: Princeton University Press, 1998), 251-8.

Chapter 9: Pseudo-Problems and Pseudo-Solutions

1 It may be asked, "How can a reform deal with both a pseudo-problem and a real problem?" The answer is that many problems are complex: big problems contain a number of smaller problems, some of which are real and some of which are illusory. For example, making ends meet is a real problem for most households. Part of this problem, for many households, is keeping the food budget within reason. However, for most households, deciding how much to spend on vacations in Monaco is not part of the problem. Those who think it is are addressing a pseudo-problem.

2 It is arguable (and we would argue), following this line of reasoning, that Departments of Canadian Studies have outlived their usefulness. They were created in the late 1960s and early 1970s as a counterweight to the huge influx of Americanism imported during the growth burst of Canadian universities by expatriate American professors and Canadian professors who did their graduate work in the United States.

3 There are those who make a distinction between conservatives and neo-liberals and who would describe the techies as neo-liberals rather than conservatives. Heavy-duty Protestant fundamentalist, gay-hating, anti-abortionist, family-value,

"guns-prevent-tyranny" conservatives count for little even in the United States, and almost nothing in Canada. Neo-liberalism is the conservatism of our times.

4 See James Traub, "Drive-Thru U," *The New Yorker,* 20 and 27 October 1997, 2–9.

5 Acadia University boasts of the Acadia Advantage, which is "an academic initiative unique in Canada that integrates the use of notebook computers into the under- graduate curriculum. It is an exciting undertaking that advances the teaching and learning environment. Acadia's students receive IBM ThinkPad computers for use during the academic year, and their computers become an integral part of their learning experience." <www.acadiau.ca/advantage> (10 May 1998).

6 Toronto has more than 30,000 undergraduate students, Harvard fewer than 7,000.

7 There is a good case for including the University of Calgary in this list, and some- what weaker cases for including the University of Ottawa, Simon Fraser, the Uni- versity of Saskatchewan, and York. The exact contents of the list do not affect our argument.

8 For a good discussion, see Matthew W. Finkin, ed., *The Case for Tenure* (Ithaca, NY, and London: IRL Press, 1996).

9 Actually, assistant professors are also evaluated quite carefully at the end of their sec- ond year. This gives both the candidate and the university some protection. The candidate knows whether he or she is performing well enough to receive tenure. And the university protects itself against the charge of arbitrariness in case tenure is denied.

10 This gambit is already depressingly common (and successful) among candidates for tenure.

11 John Scott Cowan, *Lessons from the Fabrikant File: A Report to the Board of Governors of Concordia University* (Montreal: Concordia University, May 1994).

12 For an *excellent* discussion of the hocus-pocus involved in babble about excellence in universities, see chapter 2 in Bill Reading's otherwise much overpraised book *The University in Ruins* (Cambridge, MA: Harvard University Press, 1996).

13 The abolition of tenure is an obvious exception. Its purpose is to enhance fairness and efficiency. Another exception is the proposal to raise tuition fees, so that stu- dents pay for a larger share of the cost of their education. The purpose of this pro- posal, too, is to enhance fairness. The idea behind it is that people with university degrees have substantially greater lifetime earnings than others and should pay part of the cost of this advantage.

Chapter 10: Real Problems, Real Solutions

1 Note that a considerable amount of social science research is conducted as part of the research programs of royal commissions. Royal commissions are invariably designed to assist the government of the day. They show very starkly that the qual- ity of research needs to be divorced from the funding of it.

2 Apparently contemporaneity as well as novelty is necessary. We are unaware of courses on passé pop culture, such as radio shows of the 1930s, vaudeville acts, or seventeenth-century Icelandic sagas.

3 Many PhD students receive graduate assistantships. That is, they receive salaries for assisting professors. Sometimes, but certainly not always, this assistance involves some teaching. Even when teaching is involved, however, it is usually neither required nor expected that anyone will give the assistant advice about teaching. It is also noteworthy that scholarships (which do not require students to assist professors) are more lucrative and more prestigious than assistantships.

4 Note that sessional lecturers are, or recently were, graduate students. Our recommendation, carried to an illogical conclusion, implies that graduate students should be taught only by other graduate students.

5 For a brilliant, though difficult, academic exploration of the view we adopt here, see Eric A. Nordlinger, *On the Autonomy of the Democratic State* (Cambridge, MA: Harvard University Press, 1981).

6 A good example is George Dennis O'Brien, *All the Essential Half Truths about Higher Education* (Chicago: University of Chicago Press, 1998).

BIBLIOGRAPHY

Anderson, Charles O. *Prescribing the Life of the Mind.* Madison: University of Wisconsin Press, 1993.

Anderson, Martin. *Impostors in the Temple.* New York: Simon and Schuster, 1992.

Arrowsmith, William. "The Future of Teaching." In *Improving College Teaching,* ed. Calvin B. Lee, 55-71. Washington, DC: American Council of Education, 1967.

Arthurs, H.W., Roger A. Blais, and Jon Thompson. *Integrity in Scholarship: A Report to Concordia University.* Montreal: Concordia University, April 1994.

Aucoin, Peter. *The New Pubic Management: Canada in Comparative Perspective.* Montreal: Institute for Research on Public Policy, 1995.

Axelrod, Paul. *Scholars and Dollars: Politics, Economics and the Universities of Ontario 1945-1980.* Toronto: University of Toronto Press, 1982.

Barber, Benjamin R. *An Aristocracy of Everyone: The Politics of Education and the Future of America.* New York: Ballantine Books, 1992.

Barzun, Jacques. *The American University: How It Runs, Where It Is Going.* 2nd ed. Chicago: University of Chicago Press, 1993.

Ben-David, Joseph. "Research and Teaching in the Universities." In *The Western University on Trial,* ed. John W. Chapman, 81-91. Berkeley: University of California Press, 1983.

Bercuson, David J., Robert Bothwell, and J.L. Granatstein. *The Great Brain Robbery: Canada's Universities on the Road to Ruin.* Toronto: McClelland and Stewart, 1984.

–. *Petrified Campus: The Crisis in Canada's Universities.* Toronto: Random House, 1997.

Birnbaum, Robert. *How Academic Leadership Works: Understanding Success and Failure in the College Presidency.* San Francisco: Jossey-Bass Publishers, 1992.

Bloom, Allan. *The Closing of the American Mind.* New York: Simon and Schuster, 1987.

Bonneau, Louis-Philippe, and J.A. Corry. *Quest for the Optimum: Research Policy in the Universities of Canada.* Vol. 1. Ottawa: Association of Universities and Colleges of Canada, 1972.

Bowen, William G., and Harold T. Shapiro. *Universities and Their Leadership.* Princeton, NJ: Princeton University Press, 1998.

Boyer Commission on Educating Undergraduates in the Research University. *Reinventing Undergraduate Education: A Blueprint for America's Research Universities.* Princeton, NJ: Carnegie Foundation for the Advancement of Teaching, 1997.

Boyer, Ernest L. *Scholarship Reconsidered: Priorities for the Professoriate.* New York: Carnegie Foundation for the Advancement of Teaching, 1990.

Buchbinder, Howard, and Janice Newsome. "Corporate University Linkages in Canada: Transforming a Public Institution." *Higher Education* 20 (1990): 355-79.

Cameron, David M. *More Than an Academic Question: Universities, Government, and Public Policy in Canada.* Halifax: Institute for Research on Public Policy, 1991.

Cameron, J.M. *On the Idea of a University.* Toronto: University of Toronto Press, 1978.

Chapman, John W. *The Western University on Trial.* Berkeley: University of California Press, 1983.

Cohen, Wesley M., Richard Florida, Lucien Randazzese, and John Walsh. "Industry and the Academy: Uneasy Partners in the Cause of Technological Advance." In *Challenges to Research Universities,* ed. Roger G. Noll, 171-200. Washington, DC: Brookings Institution, 1998.

Cole, Jonathan R., Elinor G. Barber, and Stephen R. Graubard, eds. *The Research University in a Time of Discontent.* Baltimore and London: Johns Hopkins University Press, 1994.

Commission of Inquiry on Canadian University Education. *Report.* Ottawa: Association of Universities and Colleges of Canada, 1991.

Corry, J.A. *Farewell the Ivory Tower: Universities in Transition.* Montreal and London: McGill-Queen's University Press, 1970.

–. *My Life and Work, A Happy Partnership: Memoirs of J.A. Corry.* Kingston, ON: Queen's University Press, 1981.

Cowan, John Scott. *Lessons from the Fabrikant File: A Report to the Board of Governors of Concordia University.* Montreal: Concordia University, May 1994.

Emberley, Peter C. *Zero Tolerance: Hot Button Politics in Canada's Universities.* Toronto: Penguin Books, 1996.

Feldman, Kenneth J. "Research, Productivity and Scholarly Accomplishment of College Teachers as Related to their Instructional Effectiveness: A Review and Exploration." *Research in Higher Education* 26, 3 (1987): 227-98.

Finkin, Matthew W., ed. *The Case for Tenure.* Ithaca, NY, and London: IRL Press, 1996.

Flexner, Abraham. *Universities: American, English, German.* New Brunswick, NJ: Transaction Publishers, 1994.

Gilbert, Sid. "Quality Education: Does Class Size Matter?" *Research File* 1, 1 (April 1995).

Hirsch, E.D. Jr. *Cultural Literacy: What Every American Needs to Know.* Boston: Houghton Mifflin, 1987.

Horn, Michiel. *Academic Freedom in Canada: A History.* Toronto: University of Toronto Press, 1999.

Hutchins, Robert Maynard. *The Higher Learning in America.* New Haven, CT: Yale University Press, 1936.

Jencks, Christopher, and David Riesman. *The Academic Revolution.* Garden City, NY: Doubleday, 1968.

Jones, Glen A., ed. *Higher Education in Canada: Different Systems, Different Perspectives.* New York: Garland Publishing, 1997.

Kennedy, Donald. *Academic Duty.* Cambridge, MA: Harvard University Press, 1997.

Kerr, Clark. *The Uses of the University.* 3rd ed. Cambridge, MA: Harvard University Press, 1982.

Kimball, Roger. *Tenured Radicals: How Politics Has Corrupted Higher Education.* New York: Harper and Row, 1990.

"The Knowledge Factory: A Survey of Universities." *The Economist,* 4 October 1997, 1-22.

Kolodny, Annette. *Failing the Future: A Dean Looks at Higher Education in the Twenty-first Century.* Durham, NC, and London, UK: Duke University Press, 1998.

Labinger, Jay. A. "The Science Wars and the American Academic Profession." *Daedalus* 126, 4 (1997): 201-20.

Langford, John W. "Secrecy, Partnership and the Ownership of Knowledge in the University." *Intellectual Property Journal* 6 (June 1991): 155-69.

Lee, Calvin B., ed. *Improving College Teaching.* Washington, DC: American Council of Education, 1967.

Levi, Philip C. *Concordia University Special Audit Report on Specific Accounts of the Faculty of Engineering and Computer Science.* Montreal: Concordia University, July 1994.

Lindsay, Alan W., and Ruth T. Neumann. *The Challenge for Research in Higher Education: Harmonizing Excellence and Utility.* ASHE-ERIC Higher Education Research Report, no. 8. Washington, DC: Association for Higher Education, 1988.

McKillop, A.B. *Matters of Mind: The University in Ontario, 1791-1951.* Toronto: University of Toronto Press, 1994.

Manitoba. University Education Review Commission. *Post-secondary Education in Manitoba: Doing Things Differently.* Winnipeg: University Education Review Commission, 1993.

Marchak, Patricia. *Racism, Sexism and the University: The Political Science Affair at the*

University of British Columbia. Montreal and Kingston: McGill-Queen's University Press, 1996.

Milligan, Larry. "Basic Findings from the Research Literature." Workshop 6: The Linkages between Teaching and Research. Association of Universities and Colleges of Canada Symposium, Winnipeg, November 1993.

Mintzberg, Henry. "Managing Government, Governing Management." *Harvard Business Review* (May-June 1996): 75-83.

Munroe-Blum, Heather, with James Duderstadt, and Sir Graeme Davies. *Growing Ontario's Innovation System: The Strategic Role of University Research*. Report prepared for the Government of Ontario. Toronto, 1999.

Neilson, William A., and Chad Gaffield, eds. *Universities in Crisis: A Medieval Institution in the Twenty-First Century*. Montreal: Institute for Research on Public Policy, 1986.

Newman, John Henry Cardinal. *The Idea of a University*. New York: Longmans Green, 1947.

Newsome, Janice, and Howard Buchbinder. *The University Means Business*. Toronto: Garamond Press, 1988.

Noll, Roger G., ed. *Challenges to Research Universities*. Washington, DC: Brookings Institution, 1998.

Nordlinger, Eric A. *On the Autonomy of the Democratic State*. Cambridge, MA: Harvard University Press, 1981.

O'Brien, George Dennis. *All the Essential Half-Truths about Higher Education*. Chicago: University of Chicago Press, 1998.

Pelikan, J.L. *The Idea of the University: A Reexamination*. New Haven, CT: Yale University Press, 1992.

Pocklington, Tom. "The Place of Political Science in Canadian Universities." *Canadian Journal of Political Science* 31, 4 (1998): 643-58.

Press, Eyal, and Jennifer Washburn. "The Kept University." *The Atlantic Monthly* (March 2000): 39-54.

Quebec. *Universities and the Future, Government Policy Options Regarding Quebec Universities, Consultation Paper*. Quebec: Ministère de l'Éducation, 1998.

Reading, Bill. *The University in Ruins*. Cambridge, MA: Harvard University Press, 1996.

Rosovsky, Henry. *The University: An Owner's Manual*. New York and London: W.W. Norton, 1990.

Ross, Murray. *The Way Must Be Tried: Memoirs of a University Man*. Toronto: Stoddart, 1992.

Royal Society of Canada. *Realizing the Potential: A Strategy for University Research in Canada*. Ottawa: Royal Society of Canada, 1991.

Saul, John Ralston. *The Unconscious Civilization*. Toronto: House of Anansi Press, 1995.

Schofield, John. "A Tough Sell on Campus." *Maclean's*, 10 April 2000, 73.

Slaughter, Sheila. *The Higher Learning and High Technology: Dynamics of Higher Education Policy Formation*. Albany: State University of New York Press, 1990.

Slaughter, Sheila, and Larry L. Leslie. *Academic Capitalism: Politics, Policies and the Entrepreneurial University*. Baltimore and London: Johns Hopkins University Press, 1997.

Smith, Page. *Killing the Spirit: Higher Education in America*. New York: Viking Penguin, 1990.

Solomon, Robert, and Jon Solomon. *Up the University: Recreating Higher Education in America*. New York: Addison and Wesley, 1993.

Sperber, Murray. *Beer and Circus: How Big Time College Sports Is Crippling Undergraduate Education*. New York: Henry Holt, 2000.

Storm, Christine, ed. *Liberal Education and the Small University in Canada*. Montreal and Kingston: McGill-Queen's University Press, 1996.

Sykes, Charles J. *Profscam: Professors and the Demise of Higher Education*. Washington, DC: Regnery Gateway, 1988.

Traub, James. "Drive-Thru U." *The New Yorker,* 20 and 27 October, 1997, 2-9.

Tudiver, Neil. *Universities for Sale: Resisting Corporate Control over Canadian Higher Education*. Toronto: James Lorimer, 1999.

Turk, James L., ed. *The Corporate Campus: Commercialization and the Dangers to Canada's Colleges and Universities*. Toronto: James Lorimer, 2000.

Waite, P.B. *The Lives of Dalhousie University*. Vols. 1 and 2. Montreal and Kingston: McGill-Queen's University Press, 1994 and 1998.

Wilson, H.T. *No Ivory Tower: The University under Siege*. Richmond, ON: Voyageur Publishing, 1999.

Wolff, Robert P. *The Ideal of the University*. Boston: Beacon Press, 1969.

INDEX